FOUNDATIONS OF REFORMED CHURCH POLITY

Historical Series of the Reformed Church in America
RCA 400 Series
No. 2

Foundations of Reformed Church Polity

The Rhyme and Reason of the Order

Matthew J. van Maastricht

Reformed Church Press
Grand Rapids, MI

Library of Congress Control Number: 2022930822

ISBN: 978-1-950572-24-3

Because our Reformed roots shape our present and future together, the books in the 400 Series highlight how the past *informs* the present and *grows* us into the future, as good history should. It was the late D. Ivan Dykstra, professor of philosophy at Hope College (Holland, Michigan), who used to ask his students a key question: "What do we mean by what we say when we talk about what we do?" The books in this series seek to answer that question as well as many others.

General Editor
Steven D. Pierce
Commission on History, Reformed Church in America

Managing Editor & Cover Design
Matthew Gasero
Archives, Reformed Church in America

Layout Design
Russell Gasero
Archivist Emeritus, Reformed Church in America
Wit & Intellect Publishing LLC

To the memory of Allan Janssen and George Brown, Jr.

My two church polity teachers,
to whom I am forever indebted
for their indelible impact
on the course of my life.

Historical Series of the Reformed Church in Ameirca

RCA 400 Series publications

In print

1. *Why Do We Have Archives?*, by Russell L. Gasero

2. *Foundations of Reformed Church Polity*, by Matthew van Maastricht

Forthcoming

The Reformed Church in America and the Reign of God: The Dilemmas of a Denomination, by Daniel J. Meeter

Pursuing Unity in a Divided World: The History of Ecumenism in the Reformed Church in America, by Monica Schaap Pierce

Our Reformed Church: Four Centuries of a Living Faith, by Steven D. Pierce

The Lily among the Thorns image, redesigned for the 400 Series and in recognition of the Reformed Church in America's quatercentenary (1628-2028), is an early symbol of the Dutch Reformed Church. So calamitous was the condition of our mother Church in the sixteenth century, during the eighty years of bloody struggle for religious liberties against the gigantic power of Spain, that the church took on the name of "The Church under the Cross" and adopted the symbol The Lily among the Thorns. Previous sketches include the Dutch inscription on the border: "Gelijck een lelie onder de doornen, so is mine vriendinne onder de dochteren," which is taken from the Song of Solomon (2:2): "As the lily among the thorns, so is my love among the daughters."

Contents

General Editor's Preface

Whether you have a hard copy of this book or you've downloaded it—thank you! What you have in your possession is a treasure trove of church history that will help you appreciate our denomination's rich theological rootedness, tradition, spiritual vitality, and identity.

The Reformed Church in America (RCA) is commemorating 400 years of God's faithfulness to our ministries and global partnerships (1628-2028). The RCA's first worship service took place in New Amsterdam (now New York City) 148 years before the founding of the United States. Today, we have ministries throughout North America and across the globe. We've been around for a long time, have weathered many storms, and have countless stories to tell or retell. Whether you are a member of one of our Reformed churches or someone interested in church history more broadly, I hope you enjoy learning with us and discovering ways to celebrate God's grace to us and to those who have gone before us.

Because our Reformed roots shape our present and future together, the books in the 400 Series highlight how the past *informs* the present and *grows* us into the future, as good history should. It was the late D. Ivan Dykstra, professor of philosophy at Hope College (Holland, Michigan), who used to ask his students a fundamental question: "What do we mean by what we say when we talk about what we do?" The books in this series seek to answer that question as well as many others:

- What is the Reformed Church in America?
- How is it distinctive from other Christian communities?
- Which beliefs, values, and practices stand at the heart of this communion?
- What challenges has it overcome, and how is it challenged today?
- How is it structured and governed?
- What biblical principles undergird and vitalize its ministries?
- How can its rich heritage help it move into the future?

To answer these questions, authors in this series draw from the deep well of the RCA Archives. This indispensable ministry helps preserve our church's historical memory, including official records and documents. Located at New Brunswick Theological Seminary (New Brunswick, New Jersey), the RCA Archives has given students, teachers, researchers, laity, clergy, and visitors a much-needed place for in-depth study and research.

As we commemorate our quadricentennial, we are reminded that Christianity is a history-moored faith that instructs us, helps us gain perspective, and, in the words of Frederick Buechner, is for each of us "a series of crucial, precious, and unrepeatable moments that are seeking to lead us somewhere" (*Wishful Thinking*, New York: Harper & Row, 1973, 38). While the "somewhere" has been debated over the centuries, Christian history points to God's unbending faithfulness and the reality that life has a direction—one where we are being led back to God, to our life's source, and ultimately to wholeness. Life and faith are rooted in the mystery of God's love, merging in surprising ways throughout history. What's needed are eyes that see, ears that hear, and lips that speak these historical memories into the present.

Our history wouldn't even be possible without our willingness to tell it. We are people of a story, of a spiritual experience, and we keep those memories alive—both the cherished ones and the painful ones—when we share them with others. We are standing on the shoulders of the faithful men and women who courageously followed the call to serve God's kingdom here, there, and everywhere. Ours is the story of God's *unbending faithfulness* to them, to us, and to our children—stories that hold the promise of a better world, of a brighter future.

May this book, and others within this series, inspire you on your journey.

Steven D. Pierce
General Editor

Acknowledgments

Behind every book is a group of people and a history that helped bring it to fruition. This book is no different. This work has been rolling around in my mind for years. I am grateful for the Historical Series of the Reformed Church in America and the Commission on History for providing a path for a book such as this and their encouragement to complete this. I am grateful for all the people who had a role in producing this volume, particularly James Hart Brumm, Steven Pierce, Russell Gasero, and Matthew Gasero. Naming names is always a risk, for there is always the possibility of unintentionally leaving someone out. This list is not exclusive, and dozens of people have been instrumental, in various ways, in bringing this book about.

My former students at Western Theological Seminary and New Brunswick Theological Seminary who, through their questions and wonderings, provided me the opportunity to refine my articulation of these principles and their reflection in the church order, and especially for New Brunswick Theological Seminary who continues to give me an opportunity to teach church polity to seminarians. My friends and colleagues Dustyn Elizabeth Keepers and John Yates patiently read through these chapters and provided substantive feedback to make this volume better than it would have been otherwise. I cannot speak of my gratitude for the two individuals who helped set me on this path, Allan Janssen and George Brown, Jr., who have entered the fullness Reign of God and to whom this book is dedicated.

I am incredibly grateful to the congregation I serve, the Altamont Reformed Church, for seeing value in and being willing to support a learned ministry. And finally, though certainly not least, I am filled with gratitude for my wife Marie and my son Hendrik who put up with their husband and father being preoccupied with this manuscript.

Foreword

Many might assume that polity and a church's order, at first glance, are more similar to law than they are to theology. Those people would not be alone. Upon beginning my service on the Reformed Church in America's Commission on Church Order, I must confess I wondered why a pastor would want to serve on this commission. I recall asking that very question to the wonderful pastor who began her service at the same time as I did. Her response was twofold—the church's order was something she lived and used regularly, and she wanted to contribute and improve it. This response began to start me on my journey of realizing that the church's order is much more than simply rules.

The RCA is unique among denominations in that it has a constitution. As a lawyer, my initial reaction was to treat the RCA's constitution as analogous to state and federal constitutions. However, avocationally, I relish teaching the Heidelberg Catechism to high school students. I say a modified version of the catechism's first question and answer to my children whenever I put them to bed. Upon realizing that the catechism comprised part of the RCA's constitution, I was sent on a soul-searching journey for what its inclusion might mean. I arrived the same place as the

Rev. Matthew van Maastricht—the RCA's constitution, of which its order is a part, is part of its theology.

A constitution can be understood as something that constitutes us or gives us a framework. The Rev. Matthew van Maastricht seeks to enflesh the skeletal framework of the RCA's constitution and give the reader an understanding of why it is so important. In doing that, he draws from his significant experience with both theology and polity, which are necessarily intertwined. My service on the Commission on Church Order emphasized this understanding. It is impossible to extract one from the other. Without its theological foundation, the church's order would collapse because ultimately, what constitutes the RCA and any church is Jesus Christ. Our understanding—our theology—of Christ constitutes us and gives rise to our polity. Our polity then creates structure and framework to allow us to live out our theology.

Upon now completing my term of service on the Commission on Church Order, I found in reading the Rev. Matthew van Maastricht's book that there were still things to learn. His writing piqued my interest, filled me with great emotion for the church, and deepened my conviction that an understanding of the polity and constitution of the RCA is crucial not only for church leaders but for everyone who claims membership in a Reformed Church. Elders and deacons would be wise to review this book upon commencing their service. Ministers of Word and Sacrament would be wise to review this book regularly, not only for themselves but also if they are serving within a church, with their consistories. It is only upon routine engagement with the complicated interconnections of theology and polity that the church can most fully be the church and live out its mission on earth. If we don't know what constitutes us, and maybe more importantly, why it constitutes us, we devolve and are tempted to consider the church order simply a rulebook, which gets in the way of ministry. The Rev. van Maastricht dispels this notion that a church order must be expedient or efficient by reminding the reader of its theological purpose. Indeed, as this book shows, the RCA's polity is countercultural, but certainly not contra biblical. Many of the issues facing the Reformed Church in America and the church at large would be easier to resolve with this understanding at the core of those who participate in the decisions.

In my many interactions with him, it is clear that Rev. van Maastricht cares deeply for the church. He devotes numerous hours to its service, both as a pastor of a local congregation and on a broader level. This book is a significant contribution to the church in that it seeks to guide the church in proper functioning. When one's car does not operate correctly, both the driver and the car suffers until it gets tuned up. This book, if used properly, can serve as a "tune-up" for consistories, congregations, and the Reformed Church in America as a whole. Imagine if members trusted church leaders with governance and realized their limited role in governance is intentional (page 68), so they could embrace their Christian vocation in the world. Imagine if office-bearers understood their first accountability was to Christ and not to members (page 52). Imagine if members lived out the call on page 71 to make membership less about "rights and privileges" and more about "an organic and essential belonging." For those familiar with the Heidelberg Catechism, this should immediately trigger a thought—"I am not my own, but belong...to my faithful Savior Jesus Christ." Imagine if all churches, following this central belonging which begins the catechism, broke against the prevailing tradition cited on page 29 of "the innumerable Protestant traditions and denominations continually multiplying by dividing." The familiar hymn says, "The Church's *one* foundation is Jesus Christ her Lord," and as the Preamble to the *Book of Church Order* says, "Jesus Christ is the only Head of his church." This book gives us a path for making this so. While many see polity and order as anything but the good news of Jesus Christ, the Rev. van Maastricht will convince you that this isn't so.

Even after six years working with some of the most talented and thoughtful polity and theology scholars in the Reformed Church in America, there were still things for me to learn in this book. I am convinced that is true for anyone. But, be warned, reading this book is dangerous. It may set you on the same path I started six years ago. Once you, too, discover all the interconnections of theology and polity, you will be a part of a revolution that has the potential to lead the church into what Christ is calling it to be. When you join, you likely will find the Rev. van Maastricht near the front, leading the charge. I hope to be up there with him, and I hope to see you there.

Philip J. De Koster

INTRODUCTION

"Wait...can this happen?" The question fell like an anvil in the meeting. Over the past year, the consistory had begun giving more and more authority to their Pastor Ruth. Pastor Ruth was gifted, charismatic, and a decisive leader. The Consistory found it much more efficient to give most of the decision-making power to her, with the consistory periodically evaluating her work and setting broad parameters for her. After all, who would know better who should make profession of faith than the pastor? And who would know better than the pastor who should be baptized? And the pastor knows who is best for elder and deacon, so why not have the pastor select the people who would provide the best leadership and the best alignment with the vision and mission of the church? It did make the church run more efficiently when decisions were made by one person rather than by the whole consistory.

But this last year, someone new was added to the consistory, someone who had served as an elder before and had previously been a delegate to General Synod. As part of her preparation for General Synod, Elder Carly had read the Book of Church Order, *so that she would better understand what was going on. Elder Carly found the church*

> *order interesting, not just because she liked the sense of order, but because of what the rules meant. And so in that consistory meeting, when the consistory was reviewing the performance of Pastor Ruth, Elder Carly was concerned because this didn't seem right. So she asked, "Can this happen?" Elder John, the Vice President, said, "The consistory can delegate authority as it wishes, and we have decided to delegate the authority for these things to Pastor Ruth." Elder Carly responded, "But I don't think this is quite right. I definitely don't think that this is what the church order intends."*

This story illustrates a very important concept. While some may see the church order as simply a pragmatic instruction manual to help things move easily and smoothly, the church order is, at its heart, a theological document—a church order makes substantive statements about our faith and how we understand it. The regulations in a church order do not exist simply for expediency or efficiency but for important theological reasons. To see that, though, we have to look at the foundations upon which our church order is built. To understand what the regulations in the church order do, it is important to understand their foundations to see beyond the pieces of the puzzle to the picture that the puzzle makes, and in doing so, we can see where and why each piece fits. But first, let's back up a bit and find our orientation.

The Sacred Scriptures begin with God bringing order out of chaos. One of the first things that God did when God gathered the ancient people into a nation was to bring order to their life together—and not just any order, but one that was designed to enable them to live with one another and with God. The New Testament also displays this movement; Paul not only tells the church that they are the body of Christ, but he also describes the kind of behavior that is characteristic of life in this community (the body) and the kind of behavior that can damage it. Even in the freedom of a Spirit-filled community, that "all things should be done decently and in order;"[1] not because order, as such, is the community's goal, but because their order itself has the goal of love.

Polity refers to the structure and regulation of an organized society. We might think of a form of government. The church, as a society, also has an organization and a structure; the church has a polity. This is the case whether we admit it or not, whether we recognize it or not, whether we put it into a book of order or not. It is much better to be aware of that polity and seek to understand it.

[1] 1 Cor 14:40, NRSV.

Just as anatomy and physiology study the shape and parts and dynamics of a human body, the discipline of church polity studies the shape and parts and dynamics of the church, that is, the body of which Christ is the head. Thus, church polity is a theological discipline, and a church order is a theological document. When I say that it is "theological," I mean that it is not simply something for efficiency, expediency, or simply pragmatism, but that it arises from what the church *is*—the body of Christ—and it displays what we believe about the church—even sometimes without our awareness that it does so. Therefore, to understand, write, or modify a church order faithfully, we must, first of all, understand the nature, essence, purpose, source, and goal of the church, and we do this primarily by looking at Christ, from whom the church derives all its qualities and aspects.

Further, church polity is a dialogical discipline; it takes place in the dialogue between what we believe about the church and the particular context in which we find ourselves. Church polity, as our understanding and practice of how to live together as a church, is thus constantly impacted by our social context, by our theological convictions about the church, and in particular by our understanding of how we can best live out those convictions within that context.

Church polity finds its lived expression in the form of a church order. This little book aims to help people understand the foundational assumptions on which the church order of the Reformed Church in America is built. The Preamble to the *Book of Church Order* (often abbreviated as "*BCO*") notes that "[t]he Reformed Church in America is organized and governed according to the presbyterial order." What exactly does it mean to be "governed according to the presbyterial order?" The Preamble offers several principles by which "[t]hat order is inspired and directed."[2] This book is an examination of those principles.

A brief history

Although the church has been gathering to handle matters and make decisions for millennia, the Presbyterial form of church government, as we would recognize it, finds its origin in France, Germany, and the Swiss regions in the sixteenth century. In particular, the synodical form—from which ours is a direct descendant—developed in France in 1559. The Dutch adapted this structure in Emden, Germany, in 1571. This is the

2 *Book of Church Order* (hereafter *BCO*) (Grand Rapids, MI: Reformed Church Press, 2019), Preamble, 2. Unless otherwise noted, all references to the BCO are from the 2019 edition.

origin of the Netherlands Reformed Church, the ancestor from which we are spiritual descendants. This structure was adapted to the Dutch context through the sixteenth century, and its development continued up to the Synod of Dordrecht (Dort) in1618–19. However, it is important to note that the church order created at Dort in 1619 is not judged as some pinnacle of Reformed church order. It gains its significance in some measure because it is the last in a prematurely stopped development: no National Synod was permitted to meet in the Netherlands for nearly two hundred years after that, and by that time, the Reformed churches in North America were independent from the Netherlands and fully developing their own life separate from the Netherlands Reformed Church.

The early Reformed churches in the American colonies were under the care and supervision of the Classis of Amsterdam for about one hundred fifty years. The nature of the church order in use was complex, but research has shown that it was the Dort Church Order with its predecessors,[3] but when the Plan of Union (which began the process of independence from the Classis of Amsterdam) was adopted, it specified, "We abide in all things by the Constitution of the Netherland Reformed Church, as established by the ecclesiastical regulations of the Synod of Dordrecht, Annis 1618 and 1619."[4] When the Reformed Church adopted its Constitution in 1792, it adopted the Church Order of Dort and a set of Explanatory Articles that helped apply these regulations to the American context. A significant church order revision in 1833 combined the Church Order of Dort and the Explanatory Articles into a single church order. The church made amendments regularly and even periodic total revisions, but the next landmark revision happened in 1966 when the entire church order was restructured into the form that we now have, which also introduced the Preamble in its (largely) current form.

Church polity as a theological discipline

Because the church is the body of Christ and because it derives its being and nature from him, any faithful understanding of how to order our life together can have no other proper foundation than a theological examination of the church's being and nature, and then an application of

3 Leon van den Broeke, "Flexibility or Fixed Idea: The Dort Church Order of 1619 as a Cultural Import in America, in eds., Henk Aay, Janny Venema, & Dennis Voskuil, *Sharing Pasts: Dutch Americans Through Four Centuries* (Holland, MI: Van Raalte Press, 2017), 56.

4 *Acts and Proceedings of the General Synod of the Reformed Church in America* 1771, 9 (hereafter *MGS*).

that theology to the particular details of matters involving assembling the church for worship, the proclamation of the Word, the administration of the sacraments, and the guidance of its people.

For precision and clarity in these studies, it is important to distinguish and define terms carefully and how they will be used here. Church polity is the theological study of the principles and regulations which govern churches. However, a church order is a particular set of such regulations written to govern a specific church communion/denomination. Then, a 'church order' is a particular result within the broader discipline of church polity. Thus, when you read the term 'church polity,' I'm referring to a field of study, and when you read, 'church order,' I'm referring to a specific code of regulations, most often to the *Book of Church Order* of the Reformed Church in America. As we think theologically, we will refer to Doctrinal Standards of the Reformed Church in America, which includes the Belgic Confession.

The Belgic Confession begins its article on the government of the church by saying, "We believe that this true church ought to be governed according to the spiritual order that our Lord has taught us in his Word."[5] The Scriptures, then, are the primary source for church polity. During the Protestant Reformation of the sixteenth century, church polity reforms were, perhaps, more significant even than the doctrinal ones. The Reformed branch of this reform movement always sought to restore the order and governance of the church to a practice that reflects the Scriptures and the early church. Because the Scriptures are our only rule of faith and life, no set of regulations that we produce can be considered infallible or unchangeable. Church order is always provisional because it always exists in the process of trying to apply the biblical witness to the changing needs of the varied contexts in which the church finds itself.

The ordering of the church is not like the ordering of any other society. Many other human societies prize effective and efficient management above other considerations and efficacy often aims to operate with minimal effort or fuss. This is emphatically not the case, however, with the church. A church order cannot be a theologically neutral rulebook or instruction manual because there is no such thing. Church order is a practical ecclesiology[6] in that it helps to give life—to put into practice—to that which we believe that Christ desires for the ordering of the church

5 Belgic Confession, Art. 30.

6 Ecclesiology is the field of theology that studies the church, and the term comes from the Greek word for the church—*ekklesia*.

here and now. Therefore, a church order is a theological document, through and through, and church polity is a theological discipline.

The primary source for church polity is the Scriptures, but the Scriptures do not directly set forth a church order. Instead, in the Scriptures, we discern the nature of the church, and we find or deduce some principles, values, and practices regarding how it may be best and most faithfully lived out in the world. Sometimes these principles, etc., take the form of commands, while they come as examples found in narratives at other times. Both of these are instructive for church polity. Truly, all Christian traditions claim biblical authority for their structure and order, and it would be far too narrow-visioned to claim that only one form of governance has biblical legitimacy. Our church order, of course, hinges on our interpretation of the biblical witness, just as do our other theological documents. But the fact remains that we must always look to the Scriptures as our guide and standard when we study church polity or write, amend, or apply a particular church order. As such, we also rely on the presence and activity of the Holy Spirit among us as we study the Scriptures; and we listen to the counsel of the church, both past present, as we work.

Values like efficiency, expedience, and even efficacy cannot be the primary values that drive church polity or the formation of a church order. Presbyterial order is quite possibly the most inefficient form of church organization. However, it is a form of church organization and governance that is faithful to the biblical witness and what the Reformed believe about the church.

No particular church's order descended directly from heaven; it is always the result of a historical progression. Understanding this progression can help us gain insight both about the shoulders upon which we stand and the purposes of particular regulations. By looking at the historical placement of a regulation, and its change over time, we can also see how regulations have responded to changing circumstances. By tracing the background of particular regulations through history, we can better understand what they are for and what they are trying to do.

Because the Scriptures do not contain a fully formed church order, one of the tasks of the church is the writing of church orders. Church order is not written for a hypothetical church, or an idealized church, or a church of another place or time, but for the particular church at hand as it exists in the world. As a discipline, church polity takes the biblical witness and seeks to apply it to the church's circumstances. Although the Scriptures do not change, the circumstances do, and the church order must adapt its order, directed by the Scriptures, to give order and stru to *this* church in *this* context.

In writing about the church order that can be seen in the New Testament, the Swiss New Testament scholar Eduard Schweizer noted, "There is no such thing as *the* New Testament Church order."[7] Instead, the pieces of church orders that we do see in the New Testament are unique to their contexts. Schweizer continues,

> This does not mean, however, that Church order is a matter of indifference, or is to be dictated simply by the existing practical, political, or economic conditions. The New Testament's pronouncements on Church order are to be read as a *gospel*—that is, Church order is to be regarded as a part of the proclamation in which the Church's witness is expressed, as it is in its preaching.... So when we ask about the Church's order, we must also try to understand the Church's essential nature.[8]

This is the purpose of this book: to think deeper about the church's nature in approaching the church order.

This book will not give an exposition of or commentary on the *Book of Church Order*: for that purpose *Constitutional Theology* by Allan Janssen (now in its second edition) is an indispensable volume. Instead, the aim is to move below the church order itself into the theological and practical foundations upon which it is built. By understanding these foundations, we can begin to see the logic of the order and so also begin to understand what the church order is trying to do, or at least to understand that to which it is trying to give expression. The goal, then, is for this book to be read alongside *Constitutional Theology,* or perhaps as a preface to it.

I have tried throughout this work to use ecclesiastical rather than academic language. I have also attempted to make this work as accessible as possible. Of course, even "accessibility" is a somewhat flexible term, and I hope you will forgive me if some parts still seem opaque. A glossary of terms is included in an appendix, which can offer assistance. A second appendix contains discussion questions for each chapter, making this book useful in a group setting. Finally, a third appendix includes a discussion of the hermeneutics of church polity, which moves a little deeper into discussing how we interpret the church order.

The principles discussed here are not discrete items that follow like beads on a string but are interconnected, more akin to a web or a Celtic

7 Eduard Schweizer, *Church Order in the New Testament* (London: SCM, 1961), 13.
8 Schweizer, *Church Order*, 14–15.

e principles weaves its way through the others. The
hat appear to be redundancies in the chapters. These
s but connection points—echoes—of the other prin-
show how presbyterial polity is not simply a collection
complete whole, a net that can, one may hope, safely
d support the church and enable it to more fully "carry out the mission of its Head—to announce the good news of [Christ's] Saviorhood and extend his Lordship throughout the world."[9]

Nuts-'n'-bolts preliminaries

Before we move further, we have two critical pieces of preliminary matters to address. The first is the language of the church order; the second is the "code" to refer to the church order.

The language of church order has several distinct categories to look out for and to pay close attention to. The first is declarative language, which asserts some state of affairs to be the case. It is used for definitions (e.g., "A consistory is the governing body of a local church."[10]) or descriptions (e.g., "A consistory combines the ministerial functions and governmental powers of the offices of the minister, elder, and deacon in the service and supervision of a local church."[11]).

The second type is prescriptive language. This indicates that something is mandatory or obligatory. It is to prescribe what is to happen in a particular circumstance. Following such a rule is required, not optional. Keywords to look for are words like "shall," "must," and "should." For instance, "The consistory *shall* act in all matters calling for judgment and decision which are not specifically assigned to the board of elders or the board of deacons."[12] Another example can be seen in this regulation regarding enrollment of candidates for ministry:

> Immediately following the enrollment for a candidate for the ministry, the classis *shall* petition the General Synod on behalf of the candidate for a Certificate of Fitness for Ministry. Such a petition *must* be received a minimum of twenty-four months prior to the time it is to be given final disposition by the General Synod through its agent (the board of trustees of an RCA seminary or the Ministerial Formation Certification Agency).[13]

9 *BCO*, Preamble, 2.

10 *BCO*, 1.I.1.1.

11 *BCO*, 1.I.1.2.

12 *BCO*, 1.I.2.2, emphasis added.

13 *BCO*, 1.II.11.3, emphasis added.

These instances specify requirements that do not fall to anyone's discretion but must be followed as stated.

There is also prohibitive language in the church order, which amounts to a negative obligation, that is, it denotes a specific requirement to keep from doing something or that something specific shall not happen. Key words to look for here are "shall not," "may not," and "must not." For instance, "Elders and deacons may be re-elected, but they *shall not* be reordained to the same office."[14] It is important, then, when one sees a word like "shall" or "may" to see if it has a negative nearby, which could change the prescriptive language into a prohibition.

However, not everything is dictated, and the church order also contains permissive language. The permissive language indicates something which is allowed but not required. Look for keywords like "may" for permissive language. For instance, "A consistory *may* call a minister of a Christian church that the General Synod has declared to be in full communion with the Reformed Church in America."[15] In this instance, a consistory is not required to call such a minister, nor are they even required to consider such a minister. Still, if a minister from such a church is desired, a consistory is permitted to call a minister from there.

Finally, the church order cannot imagine all scenarios, and in some cases, it is important to give some guidance that if a given circumstance should happen, then some stated action should follow. This is the language of contingency. These keywords come in pairs, and they are often found in different parts of a sentence or a different sentence within a regulation. Therefore, it is important to read a regulation completely to see if it involves a contingency. There will be an "if" in some cases, which indicates that it applies to a contingency. For instance, when describing the process for issuing a call, the *BCO* states, "*If* the call is approved by the classis and accepted by the person called, the latter's name *shall* be published on three successive Sundays."[16] Here we can see that the latter part of this is contingent upon *both* conditions that precede it. Simply because a consistory prepares a call does not mean that the classis will approve it or that the person called will accept it. If both of these events do occur, then the prescriptive "shall" regulate what must then happen. An example where this is less clear regards the elders' responsibility to place members on the inactive list.

14 *BCO*, 1.I.2.16, emphasis added.
15 *BCO*, 1.I.2.4, emphasis added.
16 *BCO*, 1.I.2.3, emphasis added.

> [The board of elders] *shall* place on the inactive list the name of any confessing member whose relationship with the church has ceased for one year or who for one year has not made faithful use of the means of grace, especially the hearing of the Word and the use of the Lord's Supper, *unless* there are extenuating circumstances making such faithful use impossible.[17]

In this instance, the prescriptive language is modified by a contingent clause. If one only reads the first half, it seems that all people who have been apart from the congregation for a year must be placed on the inactive list, i.e., not merely *permitted* to be placed on the inactive list; they *must* be placed on the inactive list. But there is a contingency at the end, which might affect the prescriptive nature of the regulation in certain cases. Thus, it is important to read an entire regulation, not just a part of it.

A second practical preliminary matter is the "*BCO* Code," or how the *Book of Church Order* outlines its parts to help clarify its references. The *BCO* is broken into chapters, parts, articles, sections, and subsections (sometimes even sub-sub sections). Clarity and specificity are important when citing the *BCO*, and page numbers don't give enough information. Therefore it is important to cite the "code" of the specific regulation to which one is referring. This book, then, whenever it cites the *BCO*, will use a series of numbers and letters separated by periods, in the order given above of the divisions of the church order.

For example, the *BCO*'s regulation requiring that the songs used in worship be in agreement with the Doctrinal Standards is found in chapter 1, part I, article 2, section 11, subsection d. We cite this as 1.I.2.11d. If I want to cite the regulation that a consistory may invite a "minister of another denomination whose character and standard is known," which is found in chapter 1, part I, article 2, section 11, subsection e, sub-sub section 1, and will be cited as 1.I.2.11e(1). However, not every regulation is found in a subsection or even a section. Such regulation is cited with the specificity needed. For instance, if you refer to the definition of a classis, given in chapter 1, part II, article 1, it will be cited as 1.II.1. The important piece to remember is the order: chapter, part, article, section, subsection, sub-subsection. Ordinarily, the year will also be included so that we can know specifically the edition being referenced. However, in this volume, unless otherwise noted, the references are to the 2019 edition of the *BCO*.

17 *BCO*, 1.I.5.2d, emphasis added.

CHAPTER 1

Constitutionality

The Reformed Church in America (RCA) has a constitution. The requirement to have a constitution is neither self-evident nor universal. The Christian Reformed Church in North America, for instance, does not have a constitution. The presence of a constitution in the RCA is more a result of contextual circumstances in the late eighteenth century than anything else. This does not mean, however, that its presence has no significance. In this chapter, we will look at the origin of the Constitution, the constituent parts of the constitution, and how they fit together.

The Nature of the Constitution

For the first century and a half, the Dutch Reformed Church in North America was under the supervision of the Classis of Amsterdam. The church in the Netherlands was an established public church, and "we might say that the constitution of the Dutch Reformed Church in North America was still in the Netherlands."[1] The church orders from the

1 Daniel J. Meeter, *Meeting Each Other in Doctrine, Liturgy, and Government*, Historical Series of the Reformed Church in America no. 24 (Grand Rapids, MI: Eerdmans, 1993), 31.

Netherlands governed the churches. They carried with them the Belgic Confession with the Canons of Dort and the Heidelberg Catechism, along with the Liturgy from the Netherlands.[2] This three-fold structure (government, doctrine, liturgy), then, was certainly nothing new. However, to understand why these were formed into a constitution, one must remember the social and cultural contexts of the late eighteenth century. The Constitution of the United States was signed in 1787 and ratified by the requisite number of states the next year. "This was an era of constitution-making in general."[3] While we may ask why the Reformed Church has a constitution, Americans in the late eighteenth century accepted it as a matter of course. Every respectable entity had a constitution.

The Preface to the original Constitution adopted in 1792 illustrates its origins and what the Reformed Church saw itself to be doing, and we present an extended excerpt here.

> In consequence of that liberty wherewith Christ hath made his people free, it becomes their duty as well as privilege, openly to confess and worship him according to the dictates of their own consciences. To perform this aright, and to bear a proper testimony against the heresies and false opinions which have always disturbed the peace and corrupted the purity of the Church, it has been found necessary to explain with candour and boldness, the Articles of Faith and Discipline, and accurately distinguish between truth and error. Wherever such explanations constitute a bond of union wholly voluntary, and unattended with civil emoluments or penalties, they cannot be considered as an infringement upon the equal liberties of others, or as fixing boundaries and terms of communion, inimical to Christian charity. The unerring Word of God remaining the only standard of the Faith and Worship of his people, they can never incur the charge of presumption, in openly declaring, what to them appears to be the mind and will of their divine Lord and Master.
>
> The Church is a Society, wholly distinct in its principles, laws, and end, from any which men have ever instituted for civil purposes. It consists of all, in every age and place, who are chosen, effectually called, and united by faith to the Lord Jesus Christ. The different dispensations, either before, or since the coming of the Messiah, have made no essential change in the benefits of the everlasting Covenant; nor do the various denominations, or

2 Meeter, *Meeting Each Other*, 31–32.

3 Meeter, *Meeting Each Other*, 2.

> descriptions of particular Churches, under which, from many unavoidable circumstances of language, nation, or other causes of distinction, believers are classes, effect any schism in the body, or destroy the communion of saints.
>
> At the reformation it was judged proper by all the churches to ratify and publish their respective Creeds, and the adopted forms of their ecclesiastical governments. In America, since the late happy Revolution, the churches of different denominations have found it necessary to organize themselves, agreeably to the present state in which the good providence of God hath placed them, and have already published their several constitutions. The Reformed Dutch Church has been prevented by some particular circumstances from accomplishing this desirable and important object, at an earlier period. She has now completed the translations which where necessary, and presents her Constitution to the public.
>
> To the Constitution of a Church appertain its Doctrines, Mode of Worship, and Government. When these are known, its true and distinguishing character is sufficiently ascertained.[4]

The Preface continues further, but this extract helps to give us a sense of the origin of the Constitution. The final line quoted refers to the "true and distinguishing character" of the church, which is "sufficiently ascertained" when doctrine, worship, and government are known.

A constitution has to do with the enduring nature and character of a particular body. It specifies that which constitutes or makes up or forms an entity. Therefore, to change the constitution is to change the body. "The Reformed Church is a constitutional church also because it believes that the things which are in the constitution cannot be changed without changing the church itself."[5]

Because changing the constitution implies changing the church, constitutions are designed to be not easily changed, which holds true for the Constitution of the RCA. The Constitution steadies the church amid the changeable winds of momentary enthusiasms and exists specifically to prevent rapid change.

> The constitution is meant to be like the keel of a sailboat. The keel keeps the boat steady against the wind. The constitution keeps the

4 As quoted in Edward Tanjore Corwin, A *Digest of Constitutional and Synodical Legislation of the Reformed Church in America* (New York: Board of Publication of the Reformed Church in America, 1906), v–vi.

5 Meeter, *Meeting Each Other*, 13.

> Reformed church from being caught up and carried off course by whatever winds may be prevailing at the moment. The constitution is meant to do exactly what some people don't like about it: it is meant to restrict the freedom of individual interpretation of the Bible and to narrow the range of group application of the Bible.[6]

To extend the image of the keel of a sailboat—while it allows for necessary changes in course, it also holds the boat steady in the changing winds. This means that the necessary changes in course require intention, work, and time. But once a direction is set, it helps keep the direction. Some do not like the fact that constitutional change is hard and time-consuming. This difficulty, however, is not a defect. It is, in fact, part of the design.

As part of the constitution, the church order pertains to the abiding nature and course of the church, and this should prevent us from changing it for lighter matters or temporary problems (which also means that the regulations ought to be restricted only to essential matters). The church order, for instance, has the function of providing a basic framework that orders those things constitutive of the church, not for regulating other matters, however pressing, that do not, by their nature, constitute the church. Matters in that second category would fall under the purview of a code of laws which is very different in nature from a constitution. A constitution reflects the enduring character of the body. The RCA has a constitution, it does not have a code of laws.

But why do we not have a code of laws? The question is a rather complex one. The Explanatory Articles of 1793, had they not been made constitutional, could have functioned as such.[7] Constitutionality is not something that suddenly existed in the late eighteenth century; it was something that developed in the early decades. For instance, in the first half of the nineteenth century, there was significant controversy over whether a man may marry his sister-in-law after his wife dies. The General Synod had ruled that this was not permitted. And for a couple of decades defended that rule and argued that it was obligatory for the lesser assemblies to follow. However, after several years of discussion whether to eliminate it or let it stand, the General Synod rescinded the rule based in large part on the fact that "the rule...is found in resolutions only passed by General Synod at its previous sessions, and not found in the Constitution of the Reformed Protestant Dutch Church."[8] In this,

6 Meeter, *Meeting Each Other*, 165.
7 Meeter, *Meeting Each Other*, 180.
8 *MGS* 1843, 221.

we can see the understanding of constitutionality develop rather than a synodocracy (rule by a synod).

A code of regulations apart from the Constitution is certainly not impossible, and a substantial argument for a division of the Government between constitution and canons: constitution being those things which constitute the church, and canons being process and procedural regulations. This would allow the Constitution to be truly constitutional and allow for process and procedural regulations to be amended more easily.[9] In the *Church Order of the Protestant Church in the Netherlands*, the church order proper comprises about fourteen pages with approximately 170 pages of Ordinances and then 200 pages of General Regulations.[10] Therefore, a separate code of regulations is not forbidden; it is simply not how we have operated.

That being said, there are a couple of dangers in such a code of laws. The first is that there can be an increased tendency to attempt to legislate every part of the church, which is a problem because

> A church order is not intended to arrange everything down to the finest details itself. There need to be rules, but there must also be room for adaptation. Ministers and church meetings often want everything arranged in the minutest detail. It cannot be done. It is impossible to make provision for every practical circumstance and make arrangements accordingly. Ministers in particular, but members of the church council and of the congregation too, should be so thoroughly familiar with the Scriptural principles underlying the government of the church that they can manage every practical situation in the light of these principles and by making use of the existing order.[11]

A second related danger is that we may find ourselves back into the sixteenth-century church polity situation with the Canon Law of the Roman Catholic Church. A historic way to phrase this is that "God alone is Lord of the conscience, and hath left it free from the doctrines and commandments of [humans] which are in anything contrary to [God's] Word, or beside it, in matters of faith or worship."[12] This allows not

9 Meeter, *Meeting Each Other*, 178–82.

10 *Kerkorde van de Protestantse Kerk in Nederland* (Zoetermeer: Boekencentrum, 2013).

11 Pieter Coertzen, *Church and Order: A Reformed Perspective*. Canon Law Monograph Series 1 (Leuven: Peeters, 1998), 58.

12 The Westminster Confession, as quoted in PCUSA *Book of Order*, 2019–2021, F-3.0101.

complete libertarianism but rather, "that human conscience is captive to the Word of God."[13] To take a historical example, in 1522, the Swiss pastor and theologian Ulrich Zwingli preached a sermon that asserted that participation in the Lenten fast was a matter of option rather than a matter of requirement. Abstaining from meat during Lent is certainly not against Scripture; however, neither is it mandated. As such, to require it would be to go beyond the Scriptures and that "in things indifferent, Christians have the liberty to use or to abstain, and that the Church authorities have no right to forbid this liberty."[14] Any code of laws/regulations separate from the Constitution must be careful to ensure that it does not reinvent the very problem that our branch of the sixteenth-century Reformation was trying to overcome. The RCA, however, has developed without such a code, which is why we emphasize constitutionality so strongly.

In discussing the concept of constitutionality, the Commission on Theology offered this rationale for having a constitution: "the RCA's Constitution articulates how we ought to read and understand Scripture, and it embodies our shared theological values and commitments."[15] The sixteenth-century reform movement protested the existence of a code of canon law that bound above and beyond what was in the Scriptures. The constitution is authoritative, and it does bind, but it "binds the church so that it would fulfill the marks of the church."[16]

The Parts and How they Work

> Its Constitution consists of the Doctrinal Standards (which are the Belgic Confession of Faith, the Heidelberg Catechism with its Compendium, the Canons of the Synod of Dort, and the Belhar Confession), the Liturgy with the Directory for Worship, the Government of the Reformed Church in America, the Disciplinary and Judicial Procedures, this Preamble, and the Formularies.[17]

The Constitution of the Reformed Church, then, has three legs: documents that state its doctrine, liturgy, and government. This is founded upon the conviction that how we order the church, how we worship, and what we believe are all connected to one another. This structure reflects

13 Carlos E. Wilton, *Principles of Presbyterian Polity* (Louisville: Geneva, 2016), 29.

14 Philip Schaff, *History of the Christian Church* (8 vols) (reprint, Peabody, Mass: Hendrikson, 2011), 8:47.

15 *MGS* 2013, 354.

16 *MGS* 2013, 355.

17 *BCO*, Preamble, 1.

the three-fold office of Christ: Prophet (doctrine), priest (liturgy), king (government).[18]

These three legs to the Constitution are different kinds of documents that work differently in the church. In the above mentioned paper on constitutionality, the Commission on Theology identified three modes in which the Constitution operates: regulative, instructive, and redemptive. In each of these modes, all three legs are present; each mode, however, uses one of the legs more than the other. In the regulative mode, in which "we seek to order and guide (and perhaps also correct) our life together," the Government is clearly the most prominent. In the instructive mode, which "functions to teach the church, calling our attention to the biblical truths, mandates, and realities that would guide our thinking and acting," the Doctrine is clearly the most prominent operator. Finally, the redemptive mode, which "is seen when the Constitution seeks to help the people of God in their devotion to God and to reflect the love of Christ in their lives," operates most clearly in the worship and prayer life of the church, relates most closely to the Liturgy.[19]

The constitution thus consists of those documents that regulate and order the activities that constitute the church. This concept guides us to discern what is constitutional and what is not. The church is constituted by Word and sacrament, which also means that the church is not constituted by affinity, commonalities, aims, goals, or any other human contrivance. Therefore, those things which are constitutional are those things that support Word and sacrament.

Liturgy and the Constitution

The Liturgy functions primarily in the redemptive mode. The Liturgy does not function as law (which the church order does), nor is it primarily confessional (as with the Doctrine), but its goal is to "help the people of God in their devotion to God and to reflect the love of Christ in their lives."[20] The constitutional status of the Liturgy is rooted not in a legalistic compulsion to prescribe everything but in the desire to give a basic and essential structure to worship while allowing for appropriate freedom. Part of the original Preface to the Constitution offers a bit of background on why the Liturgy is constitutional.

[18] Meeter, *Meeting Each Other*, 160–2; Daniel M. Griswold, "Governing the Church," in *Church Polity, Mission and Unity: Their Impact in Church* Life, eds. Barry Ensign-George and Hélène Evers. Church Polity and Ecumenism: Global Perspectives, no. 5 (Zürich: LIT, 2019), 8-9.

[19] *MGS* 2013, 355–56.

[20] *MGS* 2013, 355.

> Her Mode of Worship is expressed in the Liturgy, where forms of several prayers are given, without any idea, however, of restraining her members to any particular terms or fixed standards for prayer. Firmly believing, that the gifts of the Holy Spirit for the edification of Zion in every age, are promised and bestowed, *the Reformed Dutch Church judges it sufficient to shew in a few specimens the tenor and manner in which public worship is performed*, and leaves it to the piety and gifts of her Ministers to conduct the ordinary solemnities of the sanctuary, in a manner they judge most acceptable to God, and most edifying to his people.[21]

In this light, we can see that the purpose of the liturgy is to show "the tenor and manner" of worship rather than ensuring that all worship is uniform. Some aspects of the Liturgy are prescribed, such as the sacramental liturgies, but the prescribed forms are the ones that support the essence of the church, that is, Word and sacrament.

A recent example of proposed changes to the Liturgy illustrates the concept of constitutionality as it applies to the Liturgy. In the conflict over differing views of human sexuality and the church, questions were raised about the constitutionality of the Liturgy. One argument was that since the Liturgy is constitutional, that would include the marriage liturgy, which spoke of marriage as between a man and a woman.[22] This led to the question of what it means that the Liturgy is constitutional and which liturgies, and which parts of them, are constitutional. The Commission on Theology noted that "orders of worship for weddings...are not constitutional."[23] This is also consistent with the historic understanding of the Reformed church. The Reformed church historian Edward Corwin noted (in his magisterial *Digest of Constitutional and Synodical Legislation)* two categories for the liturgy: obligatory forms and optional forms. The obligatory forms include: the sacramental orders, the orders for ordination, and the orders for discipline and readmission. The optional forms include: all forms of prayer, the consolation of the sick, and the marriage forms.[24] All of the obligatory forms reflect that which constitutes the church, whereas the optional forms are helpful, beneficial, and of good use in ministry but do not reflect that which constitutes the church.

The question of the constitutionality of the marriage liturgy came to the fore again in 2016 in the form of a recommendation from a task

21 Original Preface to the Constitution, 1792/3 in Corwin, *Digest*, vi. Emphasis added.

22 *MGS* 2013, 181–82.

23 *MGS* 2013, 357.

24 Corwin, *Digest*, 164.

force. The task force recommended that the RCA make a marriage liturgy to be constitutional by using the process for amending the Constitution, with the intent that adopting a marriage order "as constitutional would require its sole use as the only marriage liturgy approved for use in the RCA. Using another liturgy could lead to disciplinary action."[25] This, of course, was wrong on two fronts. The first is that there is no argument as to why marriage should be considered constitutive of the church. This recommendation would have simply shoehorned the marriage liturgy into a regulative position. Secondly, even if the marriage liturgy had somehow become constitutional, simply that status does not require its use. In fact, the sacramental liturgies are made obligatory for use not simply by being constitutional but because there is also a corresponding regulation in the church order requiring their use.

Properly speaking, a Liturgy is constitutional if and only if it clearly speaks to the essence of the church, i.e., to Word and sacrament, and enables the church to embody the marks of the church.[26]

The Doctrine and the Constitution

> The church's doctrine is most expressive of the instructive mode.
>
> In the instructive mode, the constitution functions in order to teach the church, calling our attention to biblical truths, mandates, and realities that would guide our thinking and acting. The Constitution shapes our confessing, thereby shaping us. When we use the Constitution in this way, we are intending to grow in our understanding of the gospel.[27]

The doctrinal standards state the doctrine—the teaching—of the Reformed Church.[28] The way that the Standards have functioned, however, has changed over time. The Form of Subscription, the ancestor of the current Declaration for Ministers, was rather strong in affirming the Standards. In it, the minister affirmed that they,

> do hereby sincerely, and in good conscience before the Lord, declare, by this our subscription, that we heartily believe, and are persuaded, that all the articles and points of doctrine contained in the

[25] *MGS* 2016, 82.
[26] *MGS* 2013, 355.
[27] *MGS* 2013, 355.
[28] *MGS* 2005, 91.

> Confession and Catechism of the Reformed Dutch Church, together with the explanation of some points of the aforesaid doctrine made in the National Synod, held at Dordrecht, in the year 1619, do fully agree with the Word of God. We promise, therefore, diligently to teach, and faithfully to defend, the aforesaid doctrine, without either directly or indirectly contradicting the same by our public preaching or writings. We declare, moreover, that we not only reject all errors that militate against this doctrine, and particularly those which are condemned in the above-mentioned Synod, but that we are disposed to refute and contradict them, and to exert ourselves in keeping the Church pure from such errors. And, if hereafter any difficulties or different sentiments respecting the aforesaid doctrine should arise in our minds, we promise that we will neither publicly nor privately propose, teach, or defend the same, either by preaching or writing, until we have first revealed such sentiment to the Classis, that the same may be there examined.[29]

The nature of this subscription was never uncontroversial. It also produces questions as a result of modern scholarship. Must one, for instance, affirm Mosaic authorship of the Pentateuch or Pauline authorship of Hebrews because the Confession of Faith claims it?[30] The language of "do fully agree with the Word of God" is perhaps excessively strong. And "the question has been raised whether the Government of the RCA does not place the standards on a level equal to Scripture."[31] The Commission on Theology presented a paper to the General Synod in 1971 on the role of the Standards in the church, concluding that "the authority of our standards is derived from the authority of the Scriptures and depends on their being faithful witnesses to the Word of God." As such, the Standards cannot be understood to bind in the same way that scripture binds. Secondly, "our standards must be seen as three among many witnesses to the faith."[32] As such, they do not serve as "the final word on biblical interpretation or the absolute standard of orthodox faith."[33] On this basis, the wording in the declaration was changed to "accept the Standards as historic[34] and faithful

29 Explanatory Articles, 1792, Art. 11.

30 Belgic Confession, Art. 4.

31 *MGS* 1971, 212.

32 *MGS*, 1971, 214.

33 *MGS* 1971, 215.

34 Historic not meaning old, but rather that they have a history, that they did not fall from heaven but were composed in a particular time and context and circumstances for particular needs in that time, context, and circumstance, and that in order to

witnesses to the Word of God," and this is the wording that remains to this day.

More recently, the 2018 General Synod commended a paper from the Commission on History examining this topic, and the Commission concluded,

> The understanding that led to calling our Standards "historic and faithful witnesses" clearly includes the idea that we cannot expect them to comprehend or respond to modern scientific and/or sociological situations. We also cannot bind those who read and sign the forms to be binding themselves to some strict adherence to sixteenth-century—or even late twentieth-century—concepts of sociology, science, or even theology. Nor are they meant to be disciplinary tools. Ministers, professors, and candidates are promising to engage the Standards—acknowledging their limitations—as they wrestle with the Scriptures, listening for the Word of God.[35]

As such, the confessions act as our teacher and not as another law. They set forth the doctrine upon which our tradition and church are built and with which we promise to engage. It sets guardrails to keep us from going off course rather than functioning as a straitjacket. We are to wrestle with our confessions; we are not to be imprisoned by them.

This is, of course, not a simple solution. It's not an easy answer, and it is most certainly not black and white. And this communal discernment is so important. This is why we are accountable not only to our own thoughts or opinions or views but also to the body to which we belong (the local church for members and the classis for ministers). It is for this reason that such accountability exists locally rather than with the General Synod. While the General Synod is a continuing body, it is not the same kind of body as a local church or a classis, for the General Synod does not have permanent members. With local accountability, the body is able to exercise discipline with its members, rather than a distant body making authoritative interpretations of the faith, almost as if in a vacuum, disconnected from the lived reality of the situations in which the members find themselves. This is further emphasized toward the end of chapter 2 when we discuss what is primarily meant by the term "church." It is our

understand the Standards and how to apply them today, we need to understand this to bridge the contextual gap from then to now (*MGS* 1971, 213-14).

35 *MGS* 2018, 284.

communal responsibility to be faithful to the Scriptures, to be faithful to Christ, and to listen to the Spirit, which is not only in our own hearts and minds but through the voices of others. Freedom is not easy. It would be much easier if the Standards functioned as a law. But they are not that, which does not mean they do not matter. The Standards always have the first word, and we are to discern, together, what that word is and what it means.

The Government and the Constitution

If we understand the word 'Constitution' to be a supreme law, then the Government leg of the Constitution comes closest to that. The Government (with the Preamble, the Disciplinary and Judicial Procedures, and the formularies—referred to as "the church order") most expresses the regulative mode of the Constitution which "pertains to the ordering of the church for participation in God's mission, for guiding or correcting members, officers, congregations, and assemblies."[36] Even in its regulative mode, however, the Constitution's purpose is not law for the sake of law, and certainly not anything like organizational alignment, but to help the churches to live according to its true nature as the body of Christ and thus to help form disciples of Christ.

These three modes are designed to perform different and complementary functions that all support the same end within our Constitution. How we believe, worship, and order the church are all interconnected with one another, and together, the Word is proclaimed, the sacraments are administered, and order and discipline are exercised.

A constitution is not a comprehensive code of laws which is intended to regulate all aspects of a common life. The same is true for the RCA's Constitution. The Constitution gives voice to those things which constitute the church, and is rooted in the conviction that how we believe, how we worship, and how we order ourselves are all interconnected in a rich and meaningful way. Because the Constitution has three parts, and these parts are not all the same, but operate in different "modes" expressing different aspects of the life of the church. The Constitution is not simply a legal text, but it points to the redemption which is found in Christ, it instructs us in the Christian faith, and it helps to regulate the life of the church as revealed in the Scriptures. As such, the constitution is not three

[36] *MGS* 2013, 355.

parts that function in the same way, but are three parts that function in three distinct yet interconnected ways in order to help form the people of God in a holistic manner.

CHAPTER 2

The Nature of the Church on Earth

> The church, which Scripture represents with many images, is a gathering of persons chosen in Christ through the Holy Spirit to profess faith in Jesus Christ as Lord and Savior in order to embody God's intentions for the world. Gathered by the Spirit around Word and sacrament, the church fulfills its call within the expectation of the reign of God as it participates in mission, in calling all persons to life in Christ, and in proclaiming God's promise and commands to all the world.[1]

The church is, inherently, an embodied entity. That is, the church is not an ethereal entity that exists solely in some spiritual realm, or as an ideal, whether or not we participate in the life of a local church ourselves. We hear echoes of the Confessions here, as well. The Belgic Confession speaks of the church as "a holy congregation and gathering of true Christian believers,"[2] and the Heidelberg Catechism speaks of the church

1 *BCO,* Preamble, 2.
2 Belgic Confession, Art. 27.

as "a community chosen for eternal life and united in true faith."[3] This does not mean that church only exists when people gather (e.g., for an hour on Sunday mornings), but it does mean that the church is made up of a spiritual and physical people. The church is a visible, tangible community. This is part of the reason that the Belhar Confession is so insistent about Christian unity becoming visible.[4] The church must exhibit the attributes and marks of the church in a tangible way, for the church is tangible as well as spiritual.

This also points to the fact that the church has a very briefly-stated but very universal and all-encompassing task: "to profess faith in Jesus Christ as Lord and Savior to embody God's intentions for the world." This professing, then, is not simply with our voice, as if all we do is speak. As part of our profession, we do speak, but we also profess with our lives, that is, we "embody God's intentions for the world." This embodiment, then, is the living out of our profession; it is the tangible unfolding of our profession of Jesus Christ as Lord and Savior. Allan Janssen rightly observes that our profession also displays a temporal aspect of the church, thus reflecting the Reformed confessional position that the church has existed "from the beginning of the world," as God's intentions for the world. It did not begin in 1517, or 1054, or at Pentecost, but immediately with the creation of the world, and most specifically with humankind.[5] The church, then, is not a radically new thing that recently came into being, but is "sharing in the expectation given to Israel."[6]

The church is a gathering, but not just any gathering. The church is a particular community "gathered by the Spirit around Word and sacrament." We are not the agents who form this community, nor is it formed by affinity or preference, but it is formed as it is gathered by the Spirit. This is one prime example of how the church differs from the merely voluntary societies around us. Here, we may say that the church is constituted—put together—by the Spirit and gathered around Word and sacrament. The church, then, gathers not around a charismatic leader or even around a set of shared values, principles, goals, or aspirations. More precisely, it is gathered around Jesus Christ, but in this gathering we proclaim the

3 Heidelberg Catechism, Q& A 54.

4 Belhar Confession, Art. 2.

5 Allan J. Janssen, *Constitutional Theology: Notes on the Book of Church Order of the Reformed Church in America, 2nd, ed*, Historical Series of the Reformed Church in America, no. 100. (Grand Rapids, MI: Reformed Church Press, 2019), 19; *Belgic* Confession, Art. 27; Heidelberg Catechism, Q&A 54.

6 *Kerkorde van de Protestantse Kerk in Nederland*, Article I.

gospel, so we can also say that the church gathers around pulpit, table, and font, because these are the chief ways in which Christ is proclaimed.[7]

Our commission to proclaim the gospel means that the church does not only gather together, but also scatters—and remains the church in doing so. The movement of the church is a continual gathering around pulpit, table, and font and then scattering into various communities "as it participates in mission, in calling all persons to life in Christ, and in proclaiming God's promise and commands to all the world." In this way, the church remains the salt of the earth without losing its saltiness, and the church can be the light of the world on a lampstand rather than under a basket.[8]

This proclamation, of course, is not individualistic, but it is a calling of the church, which is both personal and corporate. Moreover, the individual churches are not isolated in this, but also join with others in this task. This task is made manifest in the church order, which charges both the consistory and classis to "regularly consider... the nature and extent of the ministry [of the congregation/within classis bounds] in obedience to Holy Scripture and in response to the needs of the local community and the world."[9] We fulfill our callings, therefore, not merely as individual isolated churches, because the consistory is called to this work "in consultation with its classis." The classis is tasked to work "in consultation with its congregations." Both are to do so with their "partners in mission."[10] Thus we "regularly consider" both as individuals and as a community—locally and more broadly.

> The Reformed churches confess that the church of Jesus Christ in the world is one church, the "Holy Catholic Church." The church is the living communion of the one people of God with the one Christ who is their Head. Their oneness in him is a "communion of the saints" with Christ and with one another in the divine blessings.[11]

As stated here, the Reformed churches do not see themselves as isolated or separate from other churches, but in continuity with the "one holy catholic and apostolic Church" as is confessed universally amongst Christians in

7 The pulpit, table, and font are, of course tangible symbols which point to Word and sacrament and reference to them here does not say anything about the existence or placement of particular pieces of furniture in a worship space.

8 Matthew 5:13–16.

9 *BCO*, 1.I.2.1, 1.II.2.1.

10 *BCO*, 1.I.2.1, 1.II.2.1.

11 *BCO*, Preamble, 2.

the Nicene Creed. This point is profoundly important. Even in the time of the Protestant Reformation in the sixteenth century, the Reformed never intended to be anything other than a part of this one holy catholic and apostolic church. While we tend to have either a triumphalist view of the sixteenth-century Reformation or a critical view seeing it as overly schismatic, these views are, at the same time, both true and neither true. In speaking about the churches being divided, which, John Calvin noted, was "among the chief evils of our time," he writes to Thomas Cranmer, the Archbishop of Canterbury, "Thus it is that the members of the Church being severed, the body lies bleeding. So much does this concern me, that, could I be of any service, I would not grudge to cross even ten seas, if need were, on account of it."[12] This was a particularly important point in the Belgic Confession since part of the reason for writing the confession was to be an apology for how the Christians who call themselves Reformed did not break with the church but stood in continuity with it.

After examining the four classical attributes, we will turn to the three reformation marks and, finally, discuss what is meant by the term "church."

Classical Attributes of the Church

With the Nicene Creed, as formulated at the First Council of Constantinople (381), we confess "one, holy, catholic apostolic church." But we cannot confess, see, or live these attributes ascribed to the church except by faith, which is a gift of God working in us—the Holy Spirit. It is by the Spirit that we are united to Christ in this church. By faith, we confess Christ and his church, we see the work of Christ hidden from the world, and we live in conformity to that same work of Christ.

The church has both spiritual and earthly dimensions. Sometimes its earthly circumstances obscure the spiritual ones, thus the necessity of faith. The four classical attributes of the church in the Nicene Creed have that kind of spiritual character.

One

The church is one because Christ is one.[13] It is the body of which Christ is the head.

12 John Calvin to Thomas Cranmer, April 1552 in *Calvin: Tracts and Letters*, Vol. 5, ed. Jules Bonnet and trans. David Constable, (Philadelphia: Presbyterian Board of Publication, 1858; reprint, Carlisle, PA: Banner of Truth Trust, 2009), 347–48.

13 World Council of Churches, *The Church: Towards a Common Vision* (hereafter *The Church*), Faith and Order Paper No. 214 (Geneva: WCC Publications, 2013), §22.

This unity, of course, appears to the world to be at best a rather idealistic statement or goal and contrary to the facts we see before us. Rome and Constantinople are still divided, and as of this writing, a significant conflict remains between Constantinople and Moscow. The innumerable Protestant traditions and denominations, continually multiplying by dividing, and the various independent churches scattered around the world apparently see unity as something to avoid.

This unity was a very important concept for the Reformed of the sixteenth century, despite the institutional divisions. The Belgic Confession invites us to confess, "one single catholic or universal church."[14] Janssen notes that the confessors of the Belgic "are not about establishing an alternative church. They are claiming continuity with the church as it exists, and as it can only exist—as one."[15] Moreover, they could claim such continuity because these sixteenth-century Reformers saw their divisions not as a permanent feature of Christendom but rather as an emergency measure.[16] In the subsequent four hundred years, however, we have lost the view of Protestantism as being only an emergency measure. So the institutional unity that the sixteenth-century Reformers wanted is probably not something that we will see in the near future, precisely because we have accepted Protestantism as an acceptable enduring reality.

And yet, despite these visible circumstances, we confess—we *insist*—that the church is one, because our Lord is one. This statement of faith is not only possible but also realistic to its roots because faith is a mode of knowing, of discerning reality, even from shallow appearance.

Jesus has established an objective situation and yet has put us into a struggle to be obedient to him by conforming to it. For example, Jesus' prayer in John 17 (esp. vv. 22-23) shows the importance of unity to the life and being of the church. St. Paul's comparisons of the church to a body (Rom. 12; 1 Cor. 12) and Jesus' statement that he is the vine and his disciples are branches (John 15) show that Christians are, in fact, already objectively united to each other. And we can see the tension arise in 1 Cor. 1, which shows that the actions of Christians sometimes contradict their being. That is, the church is one, and at the same time, the church is set into a struggle to live increasingly into what it means to be one.

14 Belgic Confession, Art. 27.

15 Allan J. Janssen, *Confessing the Faith Today: A Fresh Look at the Belgic Confession.* (Eugene, OR: Wipf & Stock, 2016), 97.

16 Cornelis van der Kooi and Gijsbert van den Brink, *Christian Dogmatics: An Introduction,* trans. Reinder Bruinsma with James D. Bratt, (Grand Rapids, MI: Eerdmans, 2017), 627.

> Unity is, therefore, both a gift and an obligation for the church of Jesus Christ; that through the working of God's Spirit it is a binding force, yet simultaneously a reality which must be earnestly pursued and sought: one which the people of God must continually be built up to attain.[17]

The challenge of unity is how to live it out. It is inaccurate and too easy to say that we are spiritually united, so there's no problem. Indeed, the Belhar Confession is quite clear that unity "must become visible," that is, unity is something we work to embody tangibly. After all, the unity of the church is not just for us, but also for the world, to show the world a concord of purpose and aim as we bear witness to the good news of the grace of God in Jesus Christ. Churches are not in competition; we are all striving for a common goal. To take a word from the crest of the Reformed Church in America, this unity is *eendracht*[18] which is better translated as "concord"—many working together for a common goal and purpose.

Trying to divorce the invisible aspects of the church from its visible reality pushes one toward an over-spiritualized concept of the church that does not reflect the biblical witness on the church as a *body*. We must not sacrifice the visible for the invisible, the concrete for an abstraction. On the other hand, it is also much too easy (and inaccurate) to say that we simply need to pursue denominational mergers. Seeking structural unity beyond the local church may certainly be part of living into unity, but it is not *only* that. Unity must also be sought locally. It must be made manifest at the local level where the church is *church* most of all as it gathers around pulpit, table, and font. This applies not only to different churches of the same denomination but also to different churches of different denominations, as well as within each particular local church. Might churches come together for a common purpose such as a food pantry or to support and protect "the least of these" and advocate for justice, mercy, and peace in Christ's name? Might churches come together for worship services, including sharing the Sacrament? And, perhaps the most difficult of all, might the members of each local church see themselves as connected with each other as a matter of essence and not just an option? The ways we locally manifest unity can vary as much as the contexts in which churches and their members find themselves. The importance of our unity is not just that the visible and public unity of the churches provide a singular witness to the world; even more central to that unity is an aspect of who we are, and to live in

17 Belhar Confession, Art. 2

18 To help with understanding *eendracht*, it is helpful to think of a team of horses. It is not unity in terms of singularity, but it is unity of goal, of purpose, of aim, of labor.

contradiction of this is to deny who we are and the One who redeems and renews us.

> I therefore, the prisoner in the Lord, beg you to lead a life worthy of the calling to which you have been called, with all humility and gentleness, with patience, bearing with one another in love, making every effort to maintain the unity of the Spirit in the bond of peace. There is one body and one Spirit, just as you were called to the one hope of your calling, one Lord, one faith, one baptism, one God and Father of all, who is above all and through all and in all.[19]

Holy

The church is not only one, it is holy. "The Church is holy because God is holy. The church is holy because Christ is holy. The church is holy because the spirit of Christ, who establishes and upholds the church, is the Holy Spirit."

Again, we confess this holiness only by faith. Otherwise, we would not confess. We would only see the worldly circumstances that obscure the church's holiness, and we would have neither desire nor ability to pursue a life in holiness.

What, though, does holiness mean? Too often, we assume that holiness begins with us, that the church is a congregation and gathering of holy people. But the Belgic Confession calls the church

> a holy congregation and gathering
>   of true Christian believers,
> awaiting their entire salvation in Jesus Christ
>   being washed by his blood,
>   and sanctified and sealed by the Holy Spirit.[20]

It is, first of all, the congregation as a congregation, not merely its particular members, that are called to be holy. To understand holiness in this context, we must begin with Christ—"Christ Jesus, who became for us wisdom from God, and righteousness and sanctification and redemption."[21] The holiness of the church, at its root, is the church's organic connection with Christ. The Confession states that Christians are "awaiting their entire salvation in Jesus Christ being washed by his blood." The church is holy because, in the words of the Heidelberg Catechism, "the Son of God through his Spirit and Word, out of the entire human race, from

19 Ephesians 4:1–6, NRSV.
20 Belgic Confession, Art. 27.
21 1 Cor 1:30, NRSV.

the beginning of the world to its end, gathers, protects, and preserves for himself a community chosen for eternal life and united in true faith."[22]

But this is not all; holiness is not only an objective reality; it is both a gift that Christ claims for us and also a mode of life into which we increasingly live. We see this in the Confession that we are "sanctified and sealed by the Holy Spirit," that is, the Spirit works in us to help us to grow in holiness, to be formed more and more into the image of Christ. Holiness is commanded, as well, of God's people, that is, they are to live more fully into the holiness in which they have been claimed. "For I am the LORD who brought you up from the land of Egypt, to be your God; you shall be holy, for I am holy."[23]

The elders help the churches to live deeper into holiness. This is not legalism—or, more precisely, although it can be approached in a rigid and legalistic (and thus un-Christian) manner, holiness is also a matter of the imitation of Christ, which includes his gentleness of character even more than adherence to a law. The elders, therefore, are to be gentle guides, leading the congregation toward embodying the entire character of Christ.

> [Elders] are to study God's Word, to oversee the household of faith, to encourage spiritual growth, to maintain loving discipline, and to provide for the proclamation of the gospel and the celebration of the sacraments. They have oversight over the conduct of the members of the congregation and seek to bring that conduct into conformity with the Word of God, thereby empowering all members to live out their Christian vocation in the world. Elders exercise an oversight over the conduct of one another, and of the deacon, and of the minister/s.[24]

This can also be seen in the requirement that the board of elders is to determine if any members "need special care regarding their spiritual condition and/or are not making faithful use of the means of grace...and shall provide the means of extending Christian ministry to such persons."[25] While the board of elders can (and sadly, do) misuse their authority to be punitive and legalistic, and controlling, the office is intended to be primarily pastoral, with a shepherd staff, rather than a club. Holiness is not simply a matter within the church, but also into the members' every-day lives.

22 Heidelberg Catechism Q&A 54.
23 Lev. 11:45, NRSV.
24 *BCO*, 1.I.1.6.
25 *BCO*, 1.I.5.3.

Catholic

This word often causes a bit of confusion, for it often makes us think we are confessing the Roman Catholic Church! When we speak of Catholic with a capital 'C,' this might refer to the Roman Catholic Church. However, in the creeds, catholic is spelled with a lowercase 'c,' which refers not to Roman Catholicism, but rather to the principle of catholicity. Catholic comes from the Greek word, *katholikos*, which means 'the whole, the universal, the broad.' It means that the church has an identity or continuity throughout it that both unifies it within itself and distinguishes it from that which is not the church. For the church, that element is the person of Jesus Christ, who connects us with God by the power of the Holy Spirit. The church, therefore, is not divided by social groupings or geography or personal preferences or even by time: the church is for all people who have been gathered to Christ, its universal and unifying Head. To be "catholic," therefore, means that a given congregation has this one Head—Christ—in common with the church.

Given that people do not cease to be sinners upon their entrance to the church, the world has a hard (impossible!) task if it wants to see beyond worldly appearances. Confessing the catholicity of the church requires the gift of faith, just as one cannot confess, see, or follow Christ without faith.

The catholicity of the church, then, is not simply a pretty idea, it is very real. Our faithfulness in embodying this attribute is threatened when cultural differences (and other kinds) become a source of church *divisions*; such divisions come about when people see some criterion besides Christ as the unifying factor of the church, and thereby deny other people the recognition that they are a part of the body of Christ based on a difference around that other factor.

> Cultural and historical factors contribute to the rich diversity within the Church. The Gospel needs to be proclaimed in languages, symbols and images that are relevant to the particular times and contexts so as to be lived authentically in each time and place. Legitimate diversity is compromised whenever Christians consider their own cultural expressions of the Gospel as the only authentic ones, to be imposed upon Christians of other cultures.[26]

Divisiveness involves being distracted by legitimate diversity away from affirming Christ as the One who unites us, and this distraction, then, moves ever closer to sectarianism.[27]

26 *The Church*, §28.

27 See Belgic Confession, Art. 29.

Catholicity also points us both to the unity of the church (Christ is one, not many) and to holiness (as the character of the God we worship). This holy and undivided universality also asserts a strong connection between the local church and the broader church. That connection is, of course, Christ himself. The local church "is, in itself, a complete manifestation of the body of Christ and is subject to Christ the head of the church,"[28] but this does not mean complete autonomy or independence, for "no Reformed congregation stands by itself."[29] Said another way, the local church "is wholly Church, but not the whole Church."[30] A local church is not simply a subdivision of a broader church, but at the same time, the local church is not the fullness of the church. In other words, Christ is fully present in the local church, but he is also fully present in every other local church. And this is why the communion of local churches with others is an essential aspect of being the church, not merely an available option. Consequently, pure congregationalism risks not sufficiently embodying the catholicity of the church, because living as if the body of Christ is divided also risks denying the nature of that body. When we hold unity and catholicity together, we can see that the action of a local church is never simply an action of a single local church, because it also acts on behalf of the one, holy, catholic, and apostolic church—hereafter shortened to *One Church.* As such, congregations, while they rightly have a degree of autonomy, are never, and can never be, fully autonomous.[31]

One place in which the church manifests its catholicity is making the assemblies' geographic nature to be normative. The Church Order of Dort, for instance, speaks of the classis as "composed of neighboring churches" and the particular synod being composed of "four or more neighboring Classes."[32] While some may see this as simply a pragmatic device, it underlies a deeper theological assertion, namely that "catholicity" also means connectivity amongst people and groups who are, on the surface, unlike each other. Classes and synods often include various types of churches within their bounds: large and small churches, urban and rural churches, churches that have been established for a long time, and

28 Marry-Anne Plaatjies van Huffel, "The Relevance of Reformed Church Polity Principles: Revisiting the Concept," in *Protestant Church Polity in Changing Contexts I* eds. Allan J. Janssen and Leo J. Koffeman, Church Polity and Ecumenism: Global Perspectives, no. 2 (Zürich: LIT, 2014), 37.

29 Plaatjies van Huffel, "The Relevance of Reformed Church Polity Principles," 38.

30 *The Church*, §31.

31 Leo J. Koffeman, *In Order to Serve: An Ecumenical Introduction to Church Polity*, Church Polity and Ecumenism: Global Perspectives, no. 1 (Zürich: LIT, 2014), 108–9.

32 Church Order of Dort, 1619, Arts. 41, 47, in Corwin, *Digest*.

churches composed of first-generation immigrants. That these churches are grouped together and have to find a life together in a single classis reminds us that the church is more than us and our experience. It involves churches and people who are very different from us, that it involves Christ and *all* Christ's people. If the church is truly universal, if Christ, and not our preferences, is the One who establishes, upholds, and unites the church, then catholicity means that in our everyday practices we must hold our preferences and habits more loosely than we hold each other. That is, "catholicity" must be a tangible and not merely a conceptual aspect of the church. We must accept, with discernment, a great deal more diversity in Christ's people than we may be comfortable with. This is not simply an idealistic manifestation of the catholicity of the church, but it is a tangible one. This diversity within classes and synods can cause no minor deal of frustration and conflict, but the church's hard work consists of living into the attribute of catholicity.

Apostolic

"The Church is apostolic because the Father sent the Son to establish it. The Son, in turn, chose and sent the apostles and prophets, empowered with the gifts of the Holy Spirit at Pentecost, to serve as its foundation and to oversee its mission."[33] The apostolicity of the church, then, refers to our faithfulness to the witness of the apostles.[34] We are, as it were, disciples of Christ by being disciples of his disciples. To use another picture, we are of the school of the apostles. We work to be faithful in this school, but the fact that we are there at all and all possibility of faithfulness there is the work of the Holy Spirit.

As with the other attributes, we confess apostolicity only by faith and in our dependence on the work of the Holy Spirit. Grounding apostolicity on the Holy Spirit's work, then, means that we can't ground it in law or in a historical process, although the Holy Spirit uses these this-worldly instruments. Some traditions lodge the apostolicity of the church in what is called "apostolic succession," that is, the process in which the apostles laid hands on their successors. They, in turn, laid hands on successors, forming a line that can be traced back to the apostles. However, tightly identifying that succession with apostolicity can make apostolicity the work of a human process rather than a gift of the Holy Spirit. We consider

33 *The Church*, §22.

34 It is worth noting that the apostolic office ordinarily concluded with the apostles. The apostolicity of the church is the fidelity to the witness of the apostles, as we read in Scriptures, and has nothing to do with any modern day claims to an office or function of apostleship.

apostolicity to be the Holy Spirit's work of attaching us to the apostles in Christ, marked by the fidelity of proclamation and not a mechanistic view of apostolic succession.

Others may say that the apostolicity of the church consists in the form of institutional continuity. But we acknowledge that "faithfulness to the Gospel may at times require a break in institutional continuity."[35] Indeed, our tradition reflects such a break in institutional continuity. Although this break was not intended, it happened nonetheless through the particular circumstances of the sixteenth century. We cannot say that institutional continuity is *the* mark of faithfulness to the Gospel, but at the same time, we cannot say that institutional continuity does not matter. As a gift of the Spirit, apostolicity will not always be completely traceable by looking at worldly processes like the ordination of bishops or the continuity of institutions, as important as such processes are. Confessing it will always be a matter of faith, and living it will require significant and difficult theological reflection on the nature of the church, not simply what is expedient at any given time.

God can and does work through such tools as episcopal succession and institutional continuity. These, too, are ways in which the church may express its grateful reception of the gifts of bishops and institutions, in which it may express its faithfulness to Christ. We can also see a connection between these tools and the classis. After all, the classis functions similarly to a collegial bishop. The main responsibilities of the classis include the oversight of ministers and the oversight of consistories. The classis examines candidates for ministry, it is the body that ordains ministers, and it oversees the life and doctrine of the minister.[36] As such, the classis helps to hold the ministry of the church in continuity with the teaching of the apostles. Similarly, the classis oversees local consistories, as well, seeking to ensure that the consistory (and board of elders) maintains the apostolic witness. This can be seen, particularly in the constitutional inquiry, where the classis must engage the ministers and elder delegates of the churches to review their ministries using the questions set out in the church order.[37] The goal of that inquiry is to find any gaps that might occur in the work of the consistory, so the classis can engage the consistory to try to fill them.

The attributes of the church are seen in all spheres of the church, from the local church to the supra-denominational.

35 *The Church*, §24.

36 See *BCO*, 1.II.11, 13, 15.

37 *BCO*, 1.II.7.1.

Reformed church orders, for example, have always spoken of office-bearers as more than mere functionaries in congregational life: they are Christ-representatives called "to prepare God's people for works of service" (Eph. 4:12) and to lead them in their mission as pilgrims sent to bring good news (apostolicity). These orders have always sought to build in a measure of accountability whereby local churches were placed within a larger framework of broader assemblies (catholicity). They have insisted on entire sections devoted to church discipline, upholding wherever possible the purity of the church's life and doctrine (holiness). And they have sought to give expression to the oneness in Christ that must be experienced in every age, whether that be within the local church, specific denomination, or on the larger front of ecumenical relationships (unity).[38]

The Reformation Marks

During the Protestant Reformation of the sixteenth century, the reformers never denied any of the classical or Nicene attributes of the church. Indeed, that first generation insisted that while there was an institutional discontinuity, there was not an ecclesiological discontinuity. Although we can picture the sixteenth-century reformation as having a certain degree of triumphalism, seeing them as people who boldly broke from Rome to forge their own path, the reality was rather different. And far from forging their own paths, they were adamant that they maintained continuity. Truly, the point of the sixteenth-century reform movement was never a separate Reformed church, but to reform the *One Church.*

Therefore, they did not deny the attributes of the church as found in the creed but sought to find ways to ensure that the church reflected these attributes. It is here that we began talking about the "marks" of the true church. The Belgic Confession lists three marks, though this number is not sacrosanct. John Calvin posited two marks: pure preaching of the Gospel and pure administration of the sacraments. Theodore Beza held to only one mark: the pure preaching of the Gospel. Because the Belgic Confession identifies three marks, our tradition recognizes these three.

> The true church can be recognized
> if it has the following marks:
> The church engages in the pure preaching
> of the gospel;

38 Henry DeMoor, *Christian Reformed Church Order Commentary 2nd edition* (Grand Rapids, MI: Christian Reformed Church, 2020), 14.

it makes use of the pure administration of the sacraments
as Christ instituted them;
it practices church discipline
for correcting faults.
In short, it governs itself
according to the pure Word of God,
rejecting all things contrary to it
and holding Jesus Christ as the only Head.
By these marks one can be assured
of recognizing the true church—
and no one ought to be separated from it.[39]

These marks reflect the previous discussion of what constitutes the church: Word and sacrament, supported by church discipline.

Remember that these criteria help point to the *One Church.* As such, the marks presuppose a rather stark dichotomy: true church versus false church. They do not comprehend a more true church or a less true church. This has important consequences. First, we must be very careful in our disagreements. It is one thing to have a disagreement; it is another thing to insist that some other group is the false church. To continue from above, the true church can abide in a host of different churches and traditions and display a broad offering of legitimate diversity. Second, it is important to remember that the reform movements in the sixteenth century accepted a broad range of diversity and, with only a few exceptions, did not see one another as false churches. So we must not fall into the trap that any deviation from one's own views automatically signals the presence of a false church. It was not the case in the sixteenth century; it is not the case today. But what do these marks mean?

There is certainly a sectarian usage of these marks that insists that any deviation from an established norm crosses the boundary between the true church and the false church. Is this really what Guido de Brès, the author of the Belgic Confession, had in mind when he first penned the Confession of Faith in 1559? Emphatically not! The pure preaching of the gospel is the proclamation of the grace of God in Jesus Christ. The pure administration of the sacraments is to administer them in the way that Christ instituted them. To understand the marks of the true church here, one must contrast it with the description of the false church in that same article.

A violation of the pure preaching of the gospel is to dislocate the proper primacy of the one Word of God. Speaking or acting as if there can

39 Belgic Confession, Art. 29.

be other authorities on the same level alongside (or even which supersede) the Word threatens that primacy. This does not mean that every deviation in biblical interpretation violates the pure preaching of the gospel. Truly, interpretations that give final authority to the one Word of God, and the fullness thereof, can be said to be pure proclamations of the gospel. This is not to say that every interpretation is equally right or equally valid, but rather to say that there is room for difference, even significant difference, within the *One Church*.[40] The pure preaching of the gospel of the grace of God in Jesus Christ does not require complete uniformity of biblical interpretation.

Similarly, the pure administration of the sacraments contrasts with adding sacraments to or subtracting them from those given in Scripture or others that places more emphasis on the work of humans than on Jesus Christ. For example, although ceremonial foot-washing may be a useful and admirable practice in a church, the Scriptural basis for the practice (John 13) shows that it embodies and signifies our service to each other and reinforces humility and an attitude of mutual subordination. As useful as that is, it focuses on our habits of life and not on the work of Christ.

The "impure" administration of the sacraments, therefore, separates them in some way from Christ. And again, this does not require complete uniformity of understanding and practice of the sacraments for one to be understood to be a member of the *One Church*.

> The pure administration of the sacraments in the Belgic Confession, therefore, does not mean one particular doctrine or practice of the sacraments that marks the boundary line between the true and false church. None of the leading lights of the early Reformed tradition—not Calvin, not Farel, not Beza, not Bullinger, not à Lasco, not de Bres himself—identified the true church on the basis of such a narrow view of purity....Purity had to do with the principle of *sola scriptura*, and it was the violation of that principle, according to the Belgic Confession, that made the late medieval Roman Catholic Church a false church.[41]

40 Seung-Goo Lee, "A Biblical Theological Hermeneutics, the Pure Preaching of the Word of God, and the Unity of the Church," in *The Unity of the Church: A Theological State of the Art and Beyond*, ed. Eduardus Van der Borght, Studies in Reformed Theology 18 (Leiden: Brill, 2010), 107–8; Geerhardus Vos, *Reformed Dogmatics, Volume 5: Ecclesiology, the Means of Grace, Eschatology*, ed and trans. Richard B. Gaffin, Jr. with Kim Batteau and Allan Janssen (Bellingham, WA: Lexham Press, 2016), 26.

41 Lyle D. Bierma, "The Unity of the Church and the Pure Administration of the Sacraments," in *The Unity of the Church*, 126.

Finally, the practice of church discipline supports these other two marks. Church discipline is not intended to enforce uniformity, or 'keep people in line,' or punish people for offending the general ethos of the church. Rather, church discipline has the purpose of helping to ensure the purity of the gospel proclamation and the sacramental administration. Church discipline does not give anyone license for legalism, as it has too often been understood. Church discipline is intended to help the church grow in holiness. Remember, the church is holy because it is attached to Christ, who is holy, and so Christ both declares and enables the church to be holy. Christ, by his Spirit, continues to work in and among us to conform us to his own character, but we also respond willingly to him by seeking and working to become more like him and thus to live more fully into this holiness.

Discipline means giving attention to the shape and health of the body. Its concern is not to achieve a thorough uniformity but to maintain the integrity and health of the body. It does not seek amputation but rehabilitation. It does not seek to cut off, but to restore, not to punish, but to heal, not to cast out, but to keep in. Discipline is about restoration, not punishment. It has to do with the integrity and shape of the body. Discipline is about protecting the body.

The church order seeks in a number of ways to help the church embody these Reformation marks. Most significantly, this is lodged in the eldership. Elders "have oversight over the conduct of the members of the congregation and seek to bring that conduct into conformity with the Word of God." Elders have oversight over the entire congregation, including one another, the deacons, and the minister(s). While the minister is not amenable to the board of elders for discipline, the elders do have oversight over the conduct of the minister and ensure what the minister preaches and teaches is in accordance with the Word of God. Finally, the elders "seek to guard the sacraments of the church from being profaned."[42] From these passages, we see that the church order gives the elders a central role (even more than ministers) in helping the church embody the Reformation marks.

This, then, all leads us to the question, which is very important, but which is too often unexamined: what do we mean when we use the term "church"? To this question we now turn.

[42] *BCO*, 1.I.1.6.

What do we mean when we say "church"?

The word "church" is used in many different ways. We can speak about a building (e.g., I'm walking in front of the church), we can speak about our local congregation (e.g., I belong to this church), or we can speak about the ONE CHURCH (e.g., I believe in the holy catholic Church). And even here, we use the term church to speak in both macro and micro scales. We stated above that the local church is "wholly church but not the whole church," consequently, the attributes of the church are exhibited by the local church, but these attributes belong to the *ONE CHURCH,* of which the local church is a manifestation, as are all the others. Here, the question for us is what we mean by "church" when we speak of "the marks of the church."

The *ONE CHURCH* cannot be experienced apart from a local church. There is no concretely available "universal church" where we can participate without being somehow a part of its local tangible expression. After all, the church finds its lived and concrete expression "at the place where it manifests itself in action"[43]—that place is the local church where the faithful gather around pulpit, table, and font. So although "every local church is therefore simultaneously an independent manifestation of the body of Christ *and* part of a larger whole,"[44] the primary referent of 'church' is the local church. This is particularly important when we consider the marks of the church and how, and by whom, they are to be embodied.

By identifying these characteristics as the marks of the church, the Reformers clearly meant them to be embodied in the local church. Said another way, the denomination does not—cannot—embody the marks of the church in the way a local church can because it does not gather as a denomination around pulpit, table, and font. As such, the 'true church vs. false church' distinction is not a question, at least primarily, of denominations as it is a question about local churches. Consider the following questions: How does or can a denomination exhibit the pure preaching of the gospel? Where is the denomination's preaching? Who ensures the purity of the preaching? Or, when we think about the pure administration of the sacraments—where does the denomination administer the sacraments? Who authorizes and oversees that administration? Truly, the church is the most *church* at the local level because this is where people gather around pulpit, table, and font. This is where the gospel is

43 Herman Bavinck, *Reformed Dogmatics, Volume 4: Holy Spirit, Church, and New Creation,* ed. John Bolt and trans. John Vriend (Grand Rapids, MI: Baker Academic, 2008), 373.

44 Bavinck, *Reformed Dogmatics*, 4:374.

proclaimed and where the sacraments are administered. The local church is where discipline, ordinarily, happens because discipline centers around Word and sacrament. "Wherever Jesus Christ is present through Word and sacrament, there *is* church."[45] Therefore, when we consider the true/false church distinction, it is not, primarily, about denominations, it is about local churches. It is about local churches because, for the Reformed, the church is essentially and primarily local. The essence of the church is when the people gather around pulpit, table, and font—around Word and sacrament—supported and sustained by the offices of the church (a fuller explanation of the offices is to come below), rather than the essence of the church being at a denominational level.[46]

It is part of the essence of the church that its offices sustain Word and sacrament. Having such offices is not a discretionary but an essential matter. In fact, the definitions (for congregation, organizing church, local church, collegiate church, and multiple parish) given in the very first article of our church order all hinge on the existence of a consistory. A local church is "served and governed by a regularly constituted consistory." Still, a congregation as such does not have its own consistory: this is a somewhat fine distinction as is illustrated by the structure of a collegiate church which is a collection of congregations served by a single consistory, and so together they form one church (in modern parlance this is often called "multi-site" but is really a recovery of a very old structure of church). On the other hand, a multiple parish is a group of churches (each with a consistory) that shares its minister(s).[47]

It was noted above that "wherever Jesus Christ is present through Word and sacrament, there *is* church." This is connected to the necessity of a consistory, as well, for the elders "provide for the proclamation of the

45 Lukas Vischer, "The Church—Mother of the Believers" in *Toward the Future of Reformed Theology*, eds. David Willis and Michael Welker (Grand Rapids, MI: Eerdmans, 1999), 280.

46 One might wonder if it is possible for a denomination to be considered a false church. One could imagine a denomination that forbade the proclamation of the resurrection, for instance, in its churches; or one that required that its churches teach that Jesus was just a good person, but not divine in any real way. Could it be said that the denomination is a false church? Perhaps, and why depends on one's understanding of the church. Understanding the church in the way laid out here, we might say that the denomination would be a false church, but it would be so because *all of the churches* are required to teach and/or practice such things contrary to the Gospel and forbid conformity to the Gospel. As such, the denomination would be a false church because all of the churches therein would be false churches. Therefore, the essence of church and the true and false distinction still remains, in the first place, with the local church.

47 *BCO*, 1.I.1.1.

gospel and the celebration of the sacraments," and "guard the sacraments of the church from being profaned,"[48] while the consistory is charged with "provid[ing] services of worship" and with this, the celebration of the sacraments.[49] As such, in Reformed order, the sacraments require a board of elders to provide and oversee them.

The church is one because Christ is one, the church is holy because Christ is holy, the church is catholic because Christ is universal, the church is apostolic because the church's faith is an inheritance from the generation of apostles who received their commission directly from Christ. The marks of the church do not supplant these attributes, but help to ensure that they are embodied in the church. It is in the pure preaching of the gospel, the pure administration of the sacraments, and the practice of church discipline that the church can be a manifestation of this *One Church* which embodies these marks. Finally, when we speak of "church" we speak primarily of the local church—where the people of God hear the Word proclaimed and celebrate the sacraments—rather than the denomination. As such, the question about the church-ness is not centered at the level of the denomination but is centered in the local church.

48 *BCO*, 1.I.1.6.
49 *BCO*, 1.I.2.10–11.

CHAPTER 3

The Head of the Church

> The Reformed churches confess that Jesus Christ is the only Head of his church. The Scriptures call the church his body, and our Lord the Head of that body. He is therefore in the closest and most vital relationship to his church. As the church's true Head, he has complete authority over its life, and therefore the church must ever yield to him a ready obedience and faithfulness. Christ's headship is one of righteousness, love, and tenderness toward his people.[1]

One of the misconceptions that we need to dispel as we approach church polity is the fairly common picture of the denomination as a pyramid, with the General Synod as the top point, the regional synods below that, and then the classes, and then the local churches at the bottom. This picture does fit other denominations in which a central governing body has authority over all the other parts. This is, however, completely the opposite of how governance works in the RCA. We will talk more about this in other sections, but it is important to note that the General Synod does not sit atop the church: Christ does.

1 *BCO*, Preamble, 2.

While this may sound like the typical "Sunday school answer" (where the correct answer to any question is "Jesus"), it asserts an important, functioning principle for the government of the church. To say that Christ is the head of the church is to assert his intimate connection with all the church and that there is no living head of the church on earth. That Christ is the only head of the church is not simply a spiritual principle to which we affirm and then move on, it is a theological principle from which, in part, we derive our practice of governing.[2]

The term "head" often carries a good deal of baggage for many reasons, and, although we do need to deal with that baggage as we craft our words and practices, we nonetheless retain the term here because the biblical witness uses it to denote complexities in the relationship between Christ and the church. The importance of its lyrical use in Colossians does not lie merely in the prettiness of the language but in its ability to show us the complexity and richness of the reality to which it points: "He [Christ] himself is before all things, and in him all things hold together. He is the head of the body, the church."[3] The basic metaphor itself is simple, taking the form of a parallel analogy: "Christ" is to "church" as "head" is to "body." But that very analysis of the metaphor, in all its cold accuracy, emphasizes by its almost mechanical nature what it doesn't accomplish that the passage in Colossians does. Colossians does not merely claim analogy; it makes claims about identity and relationship. It says, "Once you have finished thinking about this, look again because there is more here." Christ, as the head of the church, is integrally and organically connected to his people, both in their being as particular members and as a community. Further, it hints at what Paul says elsewhere about the relation of each member to the whole and to each other member. Like every metaphor, this one breaks down at some point, of course, so we need to be careful that we use it in the manner we see in the Scriptures, but we do need to use it.

The gathering of the church

The church, which is also a society, is unlike any other human society. The church is not a mere voluntary society that exists by the consent of its members, a society that one may freely join or not. Rather, Christ "through his Spirit and Word, out of the entire human race, from the beginning of the world to its end, gathers, protects, and preserves

2 Pieter Coertzen, *"Decently and in Order": A Theological Reflection on the Order For, and the Order In, the Church.* Canon Law Monograph Series 4. (Leuven: Peeters, 2004), 92.

3 Col 1:17–18a, NRSV.

for himself a community chosen for eternal life and united in true faith." Therefore, the church is not gathered or preserved by the people or a universal earthly pastor, but by Christ. Because of this, those who belong to Christ are those he draws together into a body, just as your finger cannot exist and live in any meaningful way separated from your body. The Catechism states emphatically that "of this community I am and always will be a living member."[4]

The Confession of faith also states that the church does not originate from any dynamic of this world, noting that the "church has existed from the beginning of the world and will last until the end,"[5] thus implying the church preceded all of us and will out-live all of us. And because the church did not originate from the consent of the governed but from Christ, "people ought not to withdraw from [this church], content to be by themselves, regardless of their status or condition. But all people are obliged to join and unite with it."[6] We must be a part of the church not because we decide on our own to do so, but rather, as the biblical witness asserts, because God calls people together into a body; for a body to function as a body, it needs to have an organic connection. It is not possible to exist as Christians apart from the church.

The governance of the church

The image of Christ as the head of the church speaks of the profoundly complex, intense, intimate, and ultimate nature of his connection to us. Christ is "the head over all things for the church, which is his body, the fullness of him who fills all in all."[7] The head does not float above the body. To carry the organic metaphor a bit farther, we might think of the nervous system, which moves all through the body and connects every part of it with the brain. Similarly, Christ is not just in a "power-over" relationship with the church, but in an "em-powering" relationship, the source of our own being and nature, a bond in which every member serves every other member, a deeply organic union with the church.

The church gains its life from Christ and, therefore, can be neither a democracy nor a monarchy, for both of these imply that others besides Christ have authority in themselves.[8] A democracy gains its life and authority from the consent of the people who have come together;

4 Heidelberg Catechism, Q&A 54.

5 Belgic Confession, Art. 27.

6 Belgic Confession, Art. 28.

7 Eph 1:22-23, NRSV.

8 Karl Barth, *Dogmatics in Outline,* trans. G.T. Thomson (New York: Harper & Row, 1959), 146; Coertzen, *"Decently and In Order,"* 95.

a monarchy's authority flows from the monarch. The church, therefore, cannot properly be ruled by an earthly monarch or democracy. Also, in both of these, "authority" tends to operate as a variety of command-and-control.

In the church, authority consists in both conformity to truth and in using one's gifts for service. To say that Christ is the head of the church denotes his authority both because he is the truth (John 14:6) and because in serving us, he also leads us to serve each other. And because Christ has authority in this way, he also has the authority of ruling over the church. Consequently, the church must discern Christ's leading in all arenas of its life. Christ conflicts with market forces and cultural enthusiasms, and we must follow him as he does. Useful tools, like *Robert's Rules of Order*, for example, are only useful for the church to the extent that our use of them conforms to the rule of Christ. For this reason, the Reformed, traditionally, have relatively thin church orders rather than a sizable Code of Canon Law. This is not to say that order, structure, or even laws are wrong—they are necessary, for "when churches are deprived of them, their sinews disintegrate, and they are wholly deformed and scattered."[9] Rather, the Reformed decided that "this true church ought to be governed according to the spiritual order that our Lord has taught us in his Word."[10] Christ does order the church, not only as a "protest against chaos," but also by providing what is good and right for the church of Jesus Christ in the world.[11]

Christ's active direction of the church can be seen in the order as well. Meetings of the boards of elders and deacons, the consistory, the classis, the regional synod, and the General Synod stipulate that they begin and end with prayer.[12] Sometimes people see this particular requirement as strange, that we would "require" prayer. And sometimes it turns into little more than a nod to God before getting to the business. However, to begin and end with prayer is not a preparation for the meeting; it is the first and last agenda item, seeking Divine leading. After all, Christ is the head of the church, and when assemblies conduct business and make decisions, they are not charged with carrying out the will of the majority, or even the preference of the office-bearers themselves, they are to follow

9 Calvin, *Institutes of the Christian Religion*, ed. John T. McNeill and trans. Ford Louis Battles, Library of Christian Classics, no. 20 (Louisville: Westminster John Knox, 1960), IV.X.27.

10 Belgic Confession, Art. 30.

11 Barth, *Church Dogmatics*, IV/2, 677.

12 *BCO*, 1.I.4.3; 1.I.5.1; 1.I.6.3; 1.II.4.1; 1.III.4.1; 1.IV.4.1.

the leading of Christ. We trust that Christ does lead the church and guides the assembly as its members deliberate.

Who belongs?

That Christ is the head of the church also has implications for who belongs to the church. A merely voluntary society has the ability to define for themselves its membership as narrowly as it likes. However, this is not what the church is able or allowed to do. Because Christ himself gathers his church, the people of the church have neither ability nor authority to define who belongs in it and who does not. The Belhar Confession speaks to this when it proclaims that "true faith in Jesus Christ is the only condition for membership" in the church.[13] Sometimes people see this as a controversial statement, as though this makes church membership easy. However, no one can earn church membership as though it were a prize or an accomplishment.

Membership in the church results from the Holy Spirit's action of joining us to Christ. This means that our connection to other Christians is as much an objective fact as our connection to Christ (see John 15). But we can act in a manner contrary to the reality into which our Lord puts us, and such unfaithfulness has a destructive effect on our being and on the being of the church. Conforming to that reality, i.e., acting obediently and faithfully, means that we join ourselves in tangible practice to other Christians, which also takes the form of attachment to a local church body. The normal form of this is church membership, although such an attachment may take other forms. Our church order describes such membership as follows:

> [the board of elders] shall receive as confessing members of the church only those persons who have made a profession of their faith in the Lord Jesus Christ before the board of elders, or who have made a reaffirmation of a previous profession of faith, or who have presented a satisfactory certificate of transfer from another Christian church.[14]

This means that the church does not derive its nature from being like-minded people (although true attachment to Christ integrates them ever more deeply into his mind and thereby increases their likeness), nor from liking one another (although our Lord increases us in love for one another),

13 Belhar Confession, Art. 1.

14 *BCO*, 1.I.5.2b.

nor from seeing things the same way (although the Holy Spirit increasingly enables us to see our one Lord more clearly). The church does not gather because a group of people have the same missional priorities, nor do they seek alignment with any standard except the singular confession of Jesus Christ as Savior and Lord.

The famous and much-loved first question and answer to the Heidelberg Catechism says that our only comfort in life and in death is that the totality of our existence belongs to our "faithful Savior, Jesus Christ." Because we belong to Christ, we also belong to Christ's body. Membership in the church then is not faith in Christ *and* something else (e.g., faith in Christ and complete obedience to the pastor in all things; faith in Christ *and* a dress code; etc.) but only faith in Christ. Because Christ is our head, all those who belong to Christ properly belong to his church.

Christ is the head of the church, and this is not simply something nice to say, but reveals a significant reality: Christ is the only head of the church, which means that there is no head of the church on earth. Because Christ is the only head of the church, this means that we must always seek the leading of Christ—and trust that Christ does, in fact, guide the church—when seeking to make decisions. Christ as the head of the church also means that Christ is the only one who can set the bounds of who belongs to the church. The next chapter will describe the nature of authority in the church and how it derives from Christ.

CHAPTER 4

The Nature of the Church's Authority

Offices

> All authority exercised in the church is received from Christ, the only Head of the church. The authority exercised by those holding office in the church is delegated authority. Their appointment to their special tasks is by the Spirit of the Lord, and they are responsible first of all to the Lord of the church.[1]
>
> The Spiritual authority given to office-holders is exercised in the assemblies of the church. The offices meeting together represent the fullness of Christ's ministry. No office functions apart from the other offices.[2]

The Reformed Church has three governing offices: Minister of Word and Sacrament, elder, and deacon.[3] The offices of elder and minister

1 *BCO*, Preamble, 2–3.

2 *BCO*, Preamble, 3.

3 There is the fourth office of General Synod Professor, but this office is not involved in the government of the church. The Explanatory Articles of 1792 read that "all Ministers...are Bishops or Overseers in the Church" (Art. 18). This connects the minister with the bishop while noting that they are all "equal in rank and authority."

of Word and sacrament also reflect the medieval interpretation of the office of bishop, namely, to preach the Word, administer the sacraments, govern the church, and oversee its general well-being.[4] The Reformed, then, did not invent this threefold ministry but rather recovered it from its original design, thereby standing with the global church across denominational lines in understanding this threefold ministry.

The ministries of these offices are completed in Christ because Christ is the One who ultimately ministers to us materially and spiritually, into whom we are baptized, with whom we commune in the sacrament, and who is the Word proclaimed to us. These offices, therefore, arise not out of the congregation but from Christ.

The offices come *from* Christ *to* the congregation. This defines the nature of the authority exercised in these offices, in that Christ does not *transfer* his authority to us (as if it then became an attribute of the office) but exercises it himself *through* the offices as the office-bearers participate in Christ's own activity. The people who exercise those offices come from the congregation and "are made to stand opposite her, to proclaim to her, on behalf of God, the message she cannot give to herself and perhaps does not want to give either."[5] The congregation recognizes and affirms people who have appropriate gifts to function in those offices, while the authority and enablement to undertake the ministries of the office come from Christ.

Office-bearers are accountable "first of all" to Christ for their performance in their offices. This is one way the church's government differs from the representative democracy of the United States, for instance. In a liberal democracy, elected representatives represent, at least theoretically or ideally, the people, first and foremost, for they derive their authority from the people. However, office-bearers in the church derive their authority from Christ and are therefore primarily accountable to Christ. The nature of representation in the church will be discussed more in chapter six.

> The Spiritual authority given to office-holders is exercised in the assemblies of the church. The offices meeting together represent the fullness of Christ's ministry. No office functions apart from the other offices.[6]

4 World Council of Churches, *Baptism, Eucharist, and Ministry* (hereafter *BEM*), Faith and Order Paper 111 (Geneva: WCC Publications, 1982), Section on Ministry, III §20.

5 Hendrikus Berkhof, *Christian Faith: An Introduction to the Study of the Faith, Revised*, trans. Sierd Woudstra (Grand Rapids, MI: Eerdmans, 1986), 382.

6 *BCO*, Preamble, 3.

Office-bearers exercise their authority in *assemblies* and not on their own as particular persons. The four assemblies in the RCA are consistory, classis, regional synod, and General Synod. The offices gather to govern the church. "The offices meeting together represent the fullness of Christ's ministry." That is, when the minister(s), elders, and deacons meet together, they represent the fullness of Christ's ministry: the ministers teach, the elders govern, and the deacons serve. Therefore, all offices are necessary for the local church to *be* a local church, i.e., to represent the fullness of Christ's body. In the RCA, no office may be omitted. A church cannot, for instance, decide that it doesn't need to have deacons, or elders, or a minister. This is one of the reasons that a classis must appoint one of its ministers to supervise the consistory of any church that does not have an installed minister.[7] Assemblies will be discussed in more depth in chapter six.

As stated previously, offices are gifts from Christ specifically for service to the church. The Preamble notes this important point, commenting that "the ecclesiastical offices which the Reformed Church deems necessary for its ordering are understood to be essentially functional in nature, and the term 'office' is everywhere viewed in terms of service."[8] The church amended the Preamble in 1983, seemingly with no discussion at all, removing the clause "rather than of status" from the end of the final sentence. That sentence previously read, "the term 'office' is everywhere viewed in terms of service rather than of status." This was an important matter for the reform movement in the sixteenth century because at the time the Western Church frequently "made" bishops and priests without assigning them to the service of Word and sacrament.[9]

> The church members became the laity who, excluded from the government of the church and absolutely dependent for their salvation on the priest and sacraments, were left with nothing to do but listen and obey. Separated from them by a special "character" and "spirit" of office high above them are the clergy, who constitute distinct class, propagate themselves by succession, and can belong to this clerical class even without having a specific ministry within the local church.[10]

7 *BCO*, 1.II.7.3.
8 *BCO*, Preamble, 1–2.
9 Calvin, *Institutes*, IV.V.4–10.
10 Bavinck, *Reformed Dogmatics*, 4:383.

Therefore, it is important that we not see the offices as conferring status, prestige, or power, but rather as assigning responsibilities for service in the specific ministries of the church.

This identification of the office with service means that no one can be ordained to an office without having both an internal and an external "calling," i.e., having both the appropriate gifts and call from God, as well as a legitimate call from the church to a particular, concrete ministry within the church.[11] The candidate for office testifies to the internal call by affirming an internal sense that God is calling him or her toward that particular ministry. The church externally affirms that call, usually by electing the candidate to the ministry. This is why, for instance, no one can be ordained to the ministry of Word and sacrament without a call or invitation to a specific ministry,[12] and why there is no way to ordain someone to the offices of elder or deacon except for a congregation to elect them to the consistory.[13] Completing seminary studies does not automatically lead to ordination, and ordination is not simply a professional credential to which one is entitled after meeting certain requirements. The Confession of Faith is very clear about the importance of a calling:

> So all must be careful
> not to push themselves forward improperly,
> but must wait for God's call,
> so that they may be assured of their calling
> and be certain that they are
> chosen by the Lord.[14]

Similarly, office never *belongs* to the person as if it were a possession. The office always belongs to the church. The church order reflects this in several places: e.g., unlike some other denominations closely related to us (including the Presbyterian Church), office-bearers in the RCA cannot, on their own, relinquish their office. They can undoubtedly request that their ordination be removed, but to remove an ordination is the responsibility of the body conferring it. This is clearest with the minister, where the church order explicitly states that demission (the act of voluntarily relinquishing

11 Belgic Confession, Art. 31.

12 *BCO*, 1.II.13.4.

13 For someone to become a commissioned pastor, it has been the practice in some areas to "make" someone an elder in some way other than being elected to the consistory. However, it is not possible to make an elder apart from electing them to the consistory, and to do so is a radically divergent understanding of office.

14 Belgic Confession, Art. 31.

one's office) is an action of the *classis*, not the individual.[15] Similarly, the church order expects that office-bearers will continue to serve the church in the capacity of that office. One cannot stop functioning within an office and still retain that ecclesiastical office. For instance, a minister who can function within that office but does not request demission and refuses to "make satisfactory efforts" to function within that office can be charged with desertion of office.[16] No one is entitled to an office, nor is anyone entitled to retain an office. The offices always exist for particular ministries within the church; the offices always belong to Christ, and the church stewards them.

Office-bearers are not different from the members of the congregation in their essential identity. Office-bearers share in the same anointing as all believers:

> **Q. But why are you called a Christian?**
>
> A. Because by faith I am a member of Christ and so I share in his anointing. I am anointed to confess his name, to present myself to him as a living sacrifice of thanks, to strive with a free conscience against sin and the devil in this life, and afterward to reign with Christ over all creation for eternity.[17]

While office-bearers have a distinct calling, and this does differentiate them for bearing that office, they are not separated from the body of the faithful.

Therefore, although the language of "clergy" and "laity" is used within the Reformed Church, especially because it allows for some consistency of concepts amongst denominations and traditions, it is somewhat inaccurate since the Reformed have no separate clerical class that is in any essential way different from the other members of the church. Indeed, all are laity, including ministers. All are part of the *laós*—the people of God.

Types of Authority

> Their authority is of three kinds: ministerial, declarative, and spiritual. Ministerial authority is the right to act as Christ's servants. Declarative authority is the right to speak in his name within the

15 *BCO*, 1.II.15.13a.

16 *BCO*, 1.II.15.13b.

17 Heidelberg Catechism, Q&A 32.

> limits set by Scripture. The church shall declare what is in the Word and act upon it, and may not properly go beyond this. Spiritual authority is the right to govern the life and activity of the church and to administer its affairs. The church shall not exercise authority over the state, nor should the state usurp authority over the church.[18]

Authority is delegated from Christ; it is not the church's possession. It is important to consider the nature and extent of this authority that is delegated to the church from Christ. These three kinds of authority are also reflective of the three-fold office of Christ, which, again, makes sense as the church seeks to bear witness to Christ's ministry in the world meaningfully.

Ministerial authority is "the exercise of authority by those who are Christ's ministers or agents."[19] The term here does not specifically relate to the office of Minister of Word and Sacrament but more broadly to the meaning of the term 'ministry' in its aspect of servanthood. Ministry and ministerial authority have their orientation beyond themselves, specifically, toward Christ as their origin and nature and toward others as the recipients of service. The church has delegated (subordinate, derivative) authority rather than original authority, acting in Christ's name in the world.

Declarative authority "is the right to speak in his name within the limits set by Scripture." It allows us to declare, speak, proclaim in Christ's name, and teach the Word of God. This is a significant power of the church, to be able to declare in Christ's name, within the bounds of the Scriptures.

The nature of declarative authority came to the fore in 2017 when some classes sent overtures to the General Synod requesting that the General Synod exercise declarative authority by making some specified statements about same-sex marriage. They argued that declarative statements made by the General Synod are binding upon all assemblies and office-bearers in the Reformed Church. The General Synod rightly denied these overtures for the reason that "it is not within the authority of the General Synod to make this sort of declaration without making a change to the Constitution."[20]

The General Synod in 1958 also made an explicit reference to declarative authority. The report of the Committee on Ordaining Women recommended

18 *BCO*, Preamble, 3.

19 *BCO*, 1966, Preamble, 2.

20 *MGS* 2017, 151–3.

> that the General Synod make the following declarative statement: "Scripture nowhere excludes women from eligibility to the offices but always emphasizes their inclusion, prominence, and equal status with men in the church of Jesus Christ."[21]

The General Synod adopted this.[22] No one took this declarative statement by the General Synod to be binding. Women would not be broadly permitted to be ordained in all the offices for another two decades, and even then, it was not incumbent upon all classes and consistories to do so.

"Declarative authority" does not designate a specific kind of church declaration and thereby increase its authority; rather, it affirms that all church declarations have a certain *kind* of authority that we call "declarative," namely, to speak in Christ's name. The previous comments by two General Synods (2017 and 1958) illustrate that point. No church assembly moves into a special "declarative" mode, as if invoking "declarative authority" would thus give its statements more power of command than statements that did not invoke it. This sounds like the distinction between papal encyclicals and *ex-cathedra* papal statements.[23] On the contrary, the church frequently exercises declarative authority, though usually without explicitly referring to it. When the General Synod, for instance, adopted the "Revised Declaration on Holy Scripture" in 1963,[24] and when the General Synod votes to distribute a paper on the nuclear arms race to the churches in the Reformed Church in America,[25] these are examples of exercising declarative authority, even without any explicit reference to it. The church exercises declarative authority if it is saying anything at all. The nature of declarative authority is limited by the Scriptures.

Declarative authority refers to that gift from Christ to the *church* to speak *as* the church, not to a special mode of speaking that operates at one time but not at others. Declarative authority is to declare God's truth, teach, and correct. The local church exercises declarative authority when it proclaims the Gospel and when it declares forgiveness following the prayer of confession in the worship service, just as much as the General

21 *MGS* 1958, 328.

22 *MGS* 1958, 331.

23 The term *ex-cathedra* means "from the chair"—that is, from the symbolic seat of papal authority. The "Roman Pontiff, head of the college of bishops...in virtue of his office, when, as supreme pastor and teacher of all the faithful...proclaims an absolute decision a doctrine pertaining to faith or morals" is said to have made an "*ex-cathedra*" proclamation, which is understood to be infallible. These statements are, in reality, quite rare.

24 *MGS* 1963, 270.

25 *MGS* 1980, 128.

Synod does when making statements and adopting papers. The church can only declare within the bounds of the Scriptures and *cannot* go beyond it because in *attempting* to go beyond the bounds of the Scriptures, it would lose that authority. For example, the church cannot force someone to vote for a particular political candidate; neither can a church require that everyone wear purple, nor can a church forbid the eating of meat on Fridays. People may have opinions and convictions on a host of matters, but when the church speaks, the church is not allowed to go beyond or contrary to what is in the Scriptures.

"Spiritual authority" stands in contradistinction to temporal authority. The church does not run the civil government, nor does the church submit its governance to the state. Older orders have the clause, "In these assemblies, *ecclesiastical matters* only shall be transacted, and that in an ecclesiastical manner."[26] That is, the church has authority over ecclesiastical matters and only those. We can see a descendent of this regulation in our current church order, which says, "The church shall not exercise authority over the state, nor should the state usurp authority over the church." While that sounds like a thoroughly Americanized sentiment, it has much earlier roots. For example, article 36 of the Belgic Confession recognizes a distinct place for the civil government. Of course, the Belgic Confession's context differs from ours, but it nonetheless neither allows the church to be in charge of the state nor the state to be in charge of the church.

The civil government governs the affairs of the state, and the church governs the affairs of the church. "As impermissible as it is, therefore, on the one hand to assign ecclesiastical power to the civil government, it is also sinful on the other hand to change ecclesiastical power into political power."[27] This is not just because such a blending offends modern sensibilities but also because we affirm that God ordained the magistrate's office to govern civil life and the church to govern ecclesiastical life. The two dwell together: they're not entirely isolated, but they do not merge into one.

Spiritual authority also asserts the power of the church to govern its affairs. The church has the right to govern the church because God gives it that authority in Christ. The right to govern also means the right to discipline. Discipline is a profoundly unpopular word. Although it is most often understood in its negative aspect of correction or chastisement, it comes from the Latin word *disciplina,* which means instruction or teaching,

26 For instance, see 1619, Article 30; 1833, Art. 37; 1874, Art 36.

27 Bavinck, *Reformed Dogmatics*, 4:415.

which the church is enjoined to do more frequently and emphatically than to chastise. Discipline, therefore, does not merely concern punishment, as it is often understood, but also teaching, instruction, growing in discipleship. Christ thus vests the church and the church alone with the power, commission, and authority for spiritual discipleship of its members.

Because Christ is the only head of the church, all authority that the church exercises is delegated from Christ to the church, and is exercised by the offices. Offices, then, come from Christ to the congregation, and the people who function in those offices come from the congregation, and it is in this meeting that the ministry of Christ is represented in the church. The authority which is exercised by the church is of three types: declarative, ministerial, and spiritual and these three types of authority reflect the different facets of the church's ministry and the ministries of the offices: teaching, serving, and governing.

CHAPTER 5

Membership

Membership Categories and Definitions. Membership in congregations of the Reformed Church in America includes "confessing" members, "baptized" members, and "inactive" members. Reformed Church in America congregations also include "adherents."

"Confessing" members are members who have received Christian baptism and have been received by the board of elders through profession of faith, reaffirmation of faith, or presentation of a satisfactory certificate of transfer of membership from another Christian church, and who make faithful use of the means of grace, especially the hearing of the Word and the use of the Lord's Supper.

"Baptized" members are members who have received Christian baptism, who may or may not participate at the Lord's Table, and who have not been received by the board of elders as confessing members.

"Inactive" members are members who have been removed by the board of elders from the confessing membership list.

"Members" are all confessing members, baptized members, and inactive members.

> "Adherents" are all who participate in the life, work, and worship of the church, but are not members.[1]

This is a rather peculiar section to study, especially as all that it says about membership to define these four categories. As we will see, it is a later addition to the Preamble and is a bit out of place here— indeed, one may question whether this is the proper location for this. Nonetheless, it brings us to concepts of membership and what membership means, which will affect or even determine practical aspects of church life. We will look at the concept of membership and what it means in the church, the categories of membership and their meaning, and finally, what it means to be a member.

Member, Like an Arm

Membership is a versatile term for a complex of ideas. It evokes images of invitations, initiations, membership rolls, dues, rights, entitlements, benefits, being in or being out, rank and privilege, and the like. Much of that has no application whatsoever to church membership.

To understand church membership, we return to 1 Corinthians 12 and consider its metaphor of the church and its members: "Now you are the body of Christ and individually members of it."[2] Like a human body, the church is also an organic entity of parts that work together as a whole. To be a member of the church, then, is to be a part of a greater integrated whole, to have both similarities and dissimilarities to other members, and yet to work together in that whole as a unit. Being more than just the sum of its parts, the whole defines the parts anew. We are interconnected and interdependent.

To add another layer of complexity to this (and there will be more!), this "body" is not just an idea; it is as objectively real as a physical human body, although it describes the spiritual aspect of that reality more than its physical expression. However, it definitely has physical expression, which Paul elaborates in the rest of the previously-mentioned epistle.

Church membership is not only a spiritual matter (however objectively real that aspect is) having to do with the invisible and universal church. It also takes tangible, physical, concrete, particular forms in our lives, especially in the local church. The Belgic Confession calls the church a "holy assembly and congregation [that] is the gathering of those who are saved."

1 *BCO*, Preamble, 3.
2 1 Cor 12:27, NRSV.

Article 28 of the Belgic Confession describes the church as a body of people with whom Christians "are obliged to join and unite," ending with, "And so, all who withdraw from the church or do not join it act contrary to God's ordinance." [3] Christians as Christians are sometimes disobedient, not only acting contrary to a regulation but contrary to their own nature in Christ as members of a body. This does not mean that the Christian ceases thereby to be a Christian, but, as with other kinds of unfaithfulness, it means that the Christian's experience doesn't match the spiritual reality. The local church is where we experience the reality that is Christ's body. The Confession puts this in terms of duty, stating that one is obligated

> to join this assembly
> wherever God has established it,
> even if civil authorities and royal decrees forbid
> and death and physical punishment result.[4]

We experience our own identity as members of the body of Christ, by connecting ourselves to the local church, as a particular manifestation of the *One Church.*

Members of the church, then, are the parts that make up the church. None of them are more passive than others; any more than a kidney is more passive than a lung. This is why a distinction between clergy and laity is misleading because all of us have real, distinctive, and important functions in the local church's life, governance, and ministry. Truly, there is no such thing as "just a member," as in, "I'm no one special, I'm just a member," because we all stand alike as members of the church, regardless of whether one is an office-bearer, a prominent leader, or a member who serves in a less prominent position.

Categories of Membership

The *Book of Church Order* specifies three categories of membership, plus an additional not-quite-member category. In all three of the forms of membership, "member" is the noun, and "baptized," "confessing," or "inactive" is an adjective. These adjectives denote different categories of the same thing and not different things. The difference is not so much three different kinds of membership as it is three different ways to handle membership. All members are equal members of the church.

3 Belgic Confession, Art. 28.
4 Belgic Confession, Art. 28.

Baptized. Those baptized in infancy or young childhood but have not yet professed their faith before the elders are counted among the baptized members. The metaphor of the body illustrates why we include baptized children of members in the membership of the church. Membership consists of those joined to Christ and within his fellowship without regard to the ability to vote, be elected, or even understand the sermons. They belong. As they grow, they will publicly embrace the God who has already embraced them and confirm that belonging by means of their professions of faith. Affirming that children are part of the covenant fellowship also emphasizes that we, also, as adults, understand very little and are capable of very little and that belonging to Jesus Christ does not even depend upon that little but upon Christ's actions and love towards us. Indeed, in the Order for the Sacrament of Baptism, the minister says to the child,

> For you Jesus Christ came into the world;
> for you he died and for you he conquered death;
> All this he did for you, little one,
> though you know nothing of it as yet.
> We love because God first loved us.[5]

Also, after the baptism is administered, the minister declares,

> In the name of the Lord Jesus Christ,
> the only King and Head of the Church,
> *this child* of God is now
> received into the visible membership of the holy catholic Church,
> engaged to confess the faith of Christ, and
> to be God's faithful servant until life's end.[6]

As a part of the body, baptized people, even infants, are members—functioning and important parts—of the body, the church. All infants and young children who are baptized are members of the church by the baptism itself. There is no special process for making a baptized child a baptized member.

Baptism is initiation into the church, so there cannot be baptism that is not connected with membership in the church. Baptism and church membership cannot be separated from one another. It is true that when one is baptized, one is declared to be in the "visible membership of the holy catholic Church" and not just the membership of a local church. One

5 In *Worship the Lord: The Liturgy of the Reformed Church in America (Grand Rapids, MI: Reformed Church Press, 2005)* 31.

6 In *Worship the Lord*, 31–32.

is not baptized into the membership of First Reformed Church at the corner of Church and Main but rather is baptized into the holy catholic Church.

However, our obedient and faithful expression of belonging to the body is to join with others who also belong. Therefore, we express obedient and faithful membership in the *One Church* as membership in the local church. In the discussion of catholicity above, it was noted that when the local church acts, it acts on behalf of the *One Church*. This is similarly true with baptism. When the elders of a local church approve a baptism, they are not only approving a baptism for that local church or even a denomination but a baptism into the *One Church*. And as such, the elders have a weighty task.

In understanding the deep and meaningful connection between baptism and membership in the local church, this is not a matter of law but rather a matter of what it means to be the people of God. That is, those who are baptized become a part, a member, of the body, and it is essential that the body be re-membered that we might discern the body.[7] Membership most certainly has a juridical dimension, but most importantly, it means that baptism inherently carries deep and meaningful participation with a body of Christians. We could manufacture several circumstances that require discernment and decision of the board of elders, after all, the church has to do with living people, and the circumstances are as varied as there are people. The contention here is that baptism and membership belong together, that separating them contradicts their nature, and that baptized Christians are obligated to join themselves with Christ's people.

Because baptism normatively carries with it membership in the local church, the board of elders of the local church must approve all baptisms, as elders have care and oversight over the membership of their local church.[8] Baptism is not solely a private, individual, or familial matter; it is a church matter. And as a church matter, baptisms "shall be administered, if possible, at a time and place of public worship."[9] The contingent "if possible" here does not mean if preferred or if convenient; it means that the only allowable exception to baptizing at a time and place of public worship is the *impossibility* of doing so. Baptism is a matter for the *church*, it is a matter of *membership*, and it is, at the same time, membership in the *One Church*, which finds expression in membership in the local church.

7 1 Cor 11:29.

8 *BCO*, 1.I.4.2.

9 *BCO*, 1.I.2.11b.

The Belgic Confession describes what baptism means, especially as admission into the membership of the church.

> By [baptism] we are received into God's church
> and set apart from all other people and alien religions,
> that we may wholly belong to him
> whose mark and sign we bear.[10]

Confessing. This term is quite new. For most of our history, the term was "communicant," that is, those who are admitted to the Lord's Table. In fact, for most of its history, the RCA did not have a liturgical order for admission to membership but had an order for admission to the Table. This began to change in 1988 when, after a decade of discussion and study, the General Synod voted "[t]o encourage boards of elders of RCA congregations to include baptized Children at the Lord's Table."[11] This, then, required adjustments to categories of membership among other places. After all, children may not be ready for some of the responsibilities of communicant membership (such as voting at congregational meetings) and could not participate in others (such as being elected to consistory, particularly for legal reasons). The language of "communicant" no longer made sense, as there would be children who were admitted to the table but because they had not yet formally made a profession of faith were not in the communicant category of membership (even though they were, technically speaking, communicants).

In 1991, new terminology was put into the church order to distinguish between "active-confirmed members" and "unconfirmed-baptized members."[12] This term "confirmed" or "confirmation" was a relatively new official term for the Reformed Church and was used as the Reformed Church struggled with what terminology would work best. It was not long, however, before the term 'confirmation' became very problematic because 'confirmation' denotes a further action that completes—confirms—baptism, implying that "the candidate's baptism needed somehow to be completed; it wasn't enough."[13] Thus it seemed that confirmation "devalues baptism...to imply that confirmation is a completion of or a supplement to baptism." Truly, "baptism does not

10 Belgic Confession, Art. 34.

11 *MGS* 1988, 385.

12 *BCO*, 1991, Preamble, 2. This was also the first time that membership categories and definitions were placed into the Preamble to the *Book of Church Order*.

13 *MGS* 1992, 456.

need completion."[14] Rather than confirmation, the Reformed practiced profession of faith, which is "not a *kind* of confirmation, but *instead* of confirmation."[15] Given these considerations, the RCA concluded that the language of confirmation does not fit what happens in the Reformed church so that to speak of "confirmed" and "unconfirmed members" is not correct, either. In 1995, therefore, a change in terminology was proposed to speak not of "confirmed" but of "confessing" members.

> "Confessing" members then, are all persons who affirm their baptism, express repentance and faith in Christ, make faithful use of the means of grace, and submit to the discipline of the board of elders. This membership category "confessing members" acknowledges the necessity of a person signed and sealed by baptism to embrace Christ in living confession. The word "confessing" speaks of the reality which is a continuing part of the Christian's life, and discourages people from pointing to an appearance before the elders as the time of their conversion.[16]

This change was approved and was incorporated into the church order in 1996.[17]

Confessing members, then, are members who have been baptized and confess and are granted additional privileges and responsibilities, such as the ability to be elected to office and the ability to elect others to office.[18] The church is fundamentally a body that confesses Jesus Christ as Savior and Lord, so "true faith in Jesus Christ is the only condition for membership" in the church.[19]

In the same way that baptism is inextricably linked with church membership, so also is church membership inextricably linked with baptism; one cannot be baptized without becoming a member, and one cannot become a member without being baptized. If someone wishes to become a confessing member of the church but has not previously been baptized, the church also baptizes the person at a time and place of public worship. All members are baptized, though not all baptized members are confessing.

14 *MGS* 1993, 218.
15 *MGS* 1992, 459.
16 *MGS* 1995, 225–6.
17 *BCO*, Preamble, 2, 1996.
18 *BCO*, 1.I.2.14a.
19 Belhar Confession, Art. 1.

Inactive. The inactive list first appeared in the church order in 1932.[20] There are times when people drift from the congregation. Drifting from the congregation does not immediately remove someone from the body, nor should boards of elders be encouraged to remove people quickly from the membership rolls. While some view being placed on the inactive list as a punishment, it is not that at all. The point of having an inactive list is to encourage the elders to reach out to these people. The church order requires that once a member is placed on the inactive list, "the board [of elders] shall seek diligently for an additional period of one year to recover that member."[21] People who are not active in the congregation for whatever reason "remain an organic part of the congregation and are under the care and discipline of the church."[22]

Adherents. Increasingly there are people who are not members of a church or who, for whatever reason, choose not to join the church but still fully participate in the life and ministry of the church. Even though they are not members, these people are an important part of the local church and are counted in the annual report. This is more than an accounting category, however. The elders need to keep track of these people and consider them when inquiring into the congregation's spiritual health.[23] While the elders ought to care for adherents as with members, the relationship is not the same. Because they are not members, they are not formally subject to the discipline of the board of elders. They cannot vote for office-bearers or be elected to office. It is beneficial, for many reasons, for adherents to be encouraged to join the church. Still, people increasingly resist joining things. In which case, they may remain adherents for a long time.

What it means to be a member

To be a church member is to be a member of the local body (the congregation) and, by extension, the broader body (the *One Church*). However, membership in a local church gives the members a complex set of privileges and responsibilities. But also, more importantly, the shape and dynamics of this membership significantly reflect the dynamics of being a member of Christ's body, and it formalizes those dynamics.

Members have only a very limited role in the governance of the church,[24] locally or broadly (as we will explore in the next chapter). But

20 Constitution, 1932, Art VI, Sec 77.

21 *BCO*, 1.I.5.2d.

22 Janssen, *Constitutional Theology*, 25.

23 *BCO*, 1.I.5.3.

24 In fact, the only power specifically delegated to the congregation is the election of elders and deacons (See *BCO*, 1.I.2.14).

governance is not the chief dynamic within the body of Christ, and, therefore, it is not the chief dynamic within the church. Our church order frees members from having to be concerned with most governance and oversight matters so that they can embrace their Christian vocation in the world.

> Through baptism Christ calls us to new obedience:
> to love and trust God completely;
> to forsake the evil of the world; and
> to live a new and holy life.[25]

In the Order for Profession of Faith, after the elders are directed to engage prospective members in a conversation about their confession of the Christian faith and their desire to be a confessing member of the church, the church order directs the minister (or presiding elder) to ask set questions that speak to the responsibilities of church membership.

> Do you believe in one God: Father, Son and Holy Spirit; and do you confess Jesus Christ as your Savior and Lord?
> Do you accept the Scriptures of the Old and New Testaments as the only rule for faith and life?
> Do you, relying on the grace of God, promise to confess Christ publicly before others, to serve Christ daily, and to walk in Jesus' way?
> Do you promise to exhibit the joy of new life in Christ; to share fully in the life of the church; to be faithful in worship and service; and to offer your prayers and gifts?
> Do you promise to accept the spiritual guidance of the church; to walk in a spirit of Christian love with this congregation, and to seek those things which make for unity purity and peace?[26]

These questions reveal three main aspects of the responsibility and nature of membership: belief, confession, and life.

To affirm belief in the triune God and confess Christ as Savior and Lord are essential components of being a member of the Christian Church. Belief is internal, and confession is outward. Then, the first responsibility of a member is to confess outwardly this inward faith in Jesus Christ. This confession marks the church from what is not the church. Church members are called to "confess Christ publicly before others" and thereby

[25] Order for the Sacrament of Baptism, in *Worship the Lord*, 27.
[26] In *Worship the Lord*, 34–35.

to bear continual witness to the good news of the grace of God in Jesus Christ. Further, members are called to confess Christ not just with our mouths but also with our lives as we "serve Christ daily" and "walk in Jesus' way." This reveals how becoming a church member opens a door into a new way of life.

Members also have responsibilities to the church community, specifically, to "share fully in the life of the church; to be faithful in worship and service; and to offer [one's] prayers and gifts." To think that this activity in the church is merely an option that we can ignore gravely misunderstands one's nature as a member of the body of Christ and a member of this local congregation. The activities of members take many different forms, depending on the local church and the gifts of each member. Most certainly, they include regular participation in worship. Many churches also have committees, programs, and ministries that need the participation of members. These also provide excellent opportunities for members to use their gifts to build up the church and help the church live more deeply into its mission in the world. The congregation may also call upon members to serve as elders or deacons. Not every member will become an elder or deacon, and there is nothing wrong with that. However, members who receive such a call have a responsibility to consider seriously whether they also feel called by God to that ministry and office.

The complex metaphor of an organic body recognizes the presence of great diversity in the body of Christ (see Rom. 12 and 1 Cor. 12 again). Like a human body, the body of Christ needs a certain degree of diversity in order to operate at all as a body. No single person possesses the fullness of the Christian life, nor does any one person possess all the spiritual gifts. In reflecting on both the diversity and unity of the body, Paul writes,

> Indeed, the body does not consist of one member but of many. If the foot were to say, 'Because I am not a hand, I do not belong to the body,' that would not make it any less a part of the body. And if the ear were to say, 'Because I am not an eye, I do not belong to the body', that would not make it any less a part of the body. If the whole body were an eye, where would the hearing be? If the whole body were hearing, where would the sense of smell be? But as it is, God arranged the members in the body, each one of them, as he chose. If all were a single member, where would the body be? As it is, there are many members, yet one body.[27]

[27] 1 Cor 12:14-20., NRSV.

And it is for this reason that the body must be re-membered—put back together again, as the opposite of dis-membered.

Church membership has less to do with rights and privileges and far more to do with an organic and essential belonging, as with a body and its members (arms, legs, feet, hands, etc). Membership has to do with belonging to the body, and therefore, belonging to Christ. Membership is not something that is optional but something that is essential to one's faithful existence as a Christian.

CHAPTER 6

The Representative Principle

> The power which Jesus Christ bestows upon his church is mediated by the Holy Spirit to all the people. Since not everyone in the church can hold an office, and since the offices differ among themselves in function, some persons will always be subject, within the proper exercise of authority, to the decisions of others. Since the whole church cannot meet together at one time and place to deliberate, representative governing bodies must be established on the various levels. The unity of the church is preserved in acceptance of the fact that all are governed by the decisions made in their behalf by those who represent them.[1]

The representative principle is perhaps one of the most misunderstood principles identified in the Preamble, mainly because of the significant difference in meaning between representation in a liberal democracy and representation in the church. First, we will examine the question of who is representing whom, consider what elections means in light of the church, and finally, look at assemblies in light of representation, including discussions of the hierarchy of the church's structure.

1 *BCO*, Preamble, 3–4.

Who, exactly, is representing whom?

"Who is representing whom?" is a central and definitive question about representation, and this is where the meaning of the word in church government differs from that of the civil government. The meanings differ because the value systems and underlying principles differ. It must be said clearly, unequivocally, and without reservation: *the church is not a democracy.* We have touched on this previously. For many people, particularly those in nations that prize democratic ideals, this can sound like a rather shocking statement, especially because our church government so closely resembles a representative democracy in other ways. That is, we elect office-bearers (more on that next), we gather in assemblies (more on that following), and we use the term "representation." But the crux, here, is the question of who, exactly, is representing whom.

The Constitution of the United States begins, "We the people…" The governing authority, theoretically at least, originates in the people of our nation-state. It is the consent of the governed that legitimizes the government. This is reflected in a famous line from Abraham Lincoln's "Gettysburg Address," speaking of the United States government as "government of the people, by the people, and for the people." Legislative representatives, for example, are elected by the people in their legislative districts, and these districts are designed to have approximately the same number of people as other districts. This system is based on the principles that these elected officials represent people and that representation should be as nearly equal as possible.

The church, however, has very different foundations. Whereas the Constitution of the United States begins with "we the people," the Constitution of the Reformed Church declares that Christ is the only head of the church and that all authority is *delegated* from him. Therefore, while the Constitution of the United States assumes that authority rests in the people, the church never makes such a claim.

We can see examples of this in several places in the *BCO*. For instance, churches do not form themselves. The act of people coming together does not in itself make a local church. Instead, the classis is the body that forms churches,[2] and therefore only the classis can disband or dissolve churches and assume the assets and obligations of that local church.[3] Similarly, if a church wishes to transfer to a new denomination, the classis must approve and effect that transfer.[4] A church is not completely autonomous to do

2 *BCO,* 1.II.4–5.

3 *BCO,* 1.II.10.1–2.

4 *BCO,* 1.II.10.3–6

what they want to, as if the people themselves are vested with some form of original authority or power in the church. Indeed, the church is not ours, even our local church; we are simply stewards of it for a period. Similarly, ordination is conferred by the church and not claimed by any person. Because the church confers ordination,[5] only the church can undo that action. Much to the surprise of many people, individuals cannot give up their ordination all on their own. Through the classis in the case of ministers and the consistory in the case of elders and deacons, the church must take it back.[6]

The principles: 1) that Christ is the head of the church and delegates authority to the church, 2) which is exercised by the offices, and therefore 3) that church authority does not derive from the gathered community, teach us a good deal about the nature and location of power and authority in the church, and they illustrate how to understand representation.

The Preamble asserts that "The power which Jesus Christ bestows upon his church is mediated by the Holy Spirit to all the people," which is to say that the people are empowered rather than passively acted upon. This power is delegated to the whole church, not only to office-bearers. Presbyterial polity is not truly democratic, but neither is it oligarchic (rule by a few). The Preamble notes, "since not everyone in the church can hold an office...some persons will always be subject, within the proper exercise of authority, to the decisions of others." This is what sets a presbyterial form of church governance apart from a congregational one. The congregation members discern who exhibits gifts appropriate to holding office and then elect office-bearers to govern on their behalf. In this manner, the church exercises its power and delegated authority through the offices.[7] In this sense, we may say that the elders and deacons serving on the local church's consistory represent the church members, in that the office-bearers govern on behalf of the congregation.

This differs from how representatives represent their constituents in a liberal democracy. In that arrangement, the legislators stand in the stead of people to carry out the concerns and wishes of their constituency, and they are responsible chiefly to that electorate. But ecclesiastical representation does not work that way. Office-bearers in the church "are responsible first of all to the Lord of the Church." They are primarily accountable not to the people but to Christ. "The Office of Minister of Word and

5 *BCO*, 1.II.13.4–5.

6 *BCO*, 1.II.15.13a. It is true that there are not specific provisions given for the demission of elders and deacons, however it only makes logical sense for this to also apply for them, as well.

7 Vos, *Reformed Dogmatics*, 5:39.

Sacrament is one of servanthood and service representing Christ through the action of the Holy Spirit." The exact same statement is also used to describe elders and deacons.[8]

Understanding this representative principle to represent Christ on behalf of the people shifts our basic assumptions about church government away from democracy (in which the people rule) and toward a Christocracy (where Christ rules).

But what about election?

Another aspect that further confuses the matter of representation in the church (especially in contrast to liberal democracy) is election. In one way or another, the congregation elects those who will serve as elders and deacons in its consistory. In a liberal democracy, the election transmits authority: Authority is delegated to the representative from the people. Election is the authorization from the people to govern.

This is different from election in the church. Elders and deacons do not have a platform that has particular policies in it (e.g., "if you elect me, we will replace the sanctuary carpet"; "if you elect me, I will work to make sure we don't change the paint color"). Rather, "elders are chosen members of spiritual discernment, exemplary life, charitable spirit, and wisdom grounded in God's Word";[9] and "deacons are chosen members of spiritual commitment, exemplary life, compassionate spirit, and sound judgment."[10] Election in the church is not a popularity contest (though even in the church, it can become that), but the congregational affirmation that Christ has called *these* people into *those* ministries.

This is where we see internal and external dimensions to calling. A candidate needs some internal sense of being called by God to a particular ministry, and the church has to affirm that externally. Absent either of these, the church does not understand there to be a Divine call. Election, then, is an external way of affirming (or not) an internal call.

For the church's leadership to be chosen by the church itself is most certainly not new. This was one of the significant matters of contention during the sixteenth-century Protestant Reformation. In the Roman system against which they were arguing, the bishop had the role of discerning and identifying an external call. Thus churches were given priests, and the congregation had no role in affirming God's call. In Acts, however, the church grew fast enough that the apostles themselves could

8 *BCO*, 1.I.1.4, 6, 8.

9 *BCO*, 1.I.1.6.

10 *BCO*, 1.I.1.8.

not handle the workload alone, and so "the twelve called together the whole community and said..., 'friends select from among yourselves seven men of good standing, full of the Spirit and of wisdom, whom we may appoint to the work.'"[11] The community selected those whom they sensed God had called to service. The sixteenth-century Reformers argued that electing church leadership was the early church's practice and not a modern invention and that the church's practice had moved away from that shown in the Scriptures over time.[12]

The Belgic Confession affirms that the church (remember, church is primarily the local church) ought to choose its office-bearers.

> We believe that ministers of the Word of God, elders, and deacons
> ought to be chosen to their offices
> by a legitimate election of the church,
> with prayer in the name of the Lord,
> and in good order,
> as the Word of God teaches.[13]

This has been an important practice for the Reformed since the sixteenth century. The *BCO* provides different methods of holding elections for elders and deacons:

1. A double number of candidates shall be nominated by the consistory.
2. The confessing members of the congregation shall nominate and choose the whole number to be elected with or without advisory nominations by the consistory or other representatives of the congregation.
3. The method approved by the church's charter.
4. The method approved by the church's bylaws subject to approval by the classis.[14]

Although the *BCO* does not prescribe the exact way that nomination and election must happen, it does require that the election of elders and deacons be done at a congregational meeting. A church's method of election may change, but classical permission is required to change the method.[15] This means that "one task not allowed to the consistory by the

11 Acts 6:2–3, NRSV.
12 Calvin, *Institutes,* IV.IV.10–IV.V.4.
13 Belgic Confession, Art. 31.
14 *BCO*, 1.I.2.14c.
15 *BCO*, 1.I.2.14d.

church order is its self-selection. Elders and deacons are to be elected by the local congregation."[16] Election is the external call to office, and calling is *the* fundamental requirement for the ministry of the offices. Ordination follows this as a public authorization or acknowledgment of one's call. As such, "those who hold office are *responsive* to the congregation, but *responsible* to Christ alone in the exercise of their office."[17]

Assemblies

The individual office-bearers may not exercise their office independently but only together, collectively: they gather to make decisions. Office is always exercised in a collegial form.

> The Spiritual authority given to office-holders is exercised in the assemblies of the church. The offices meeting together represent the fullness of Christ's ministry. No office functions apart from the other offices. Reformed governance understands that the greater assemblies care for the ministry that extends beyond the purview of the lesser assemblies without infringing upon the responsibilities of the lesser. Consistories, classes, and synods work together in mission and ministry within their shared boundaries.[18]

This is another aspect of the nature of the church's authority. The discussion here connects the previous questions about representation with the nature of assemblies.

Assemblies and representation

The church's representative principle not only asserts whence office-bearers derive their authority but also how they exercise it: the church governs itself in assemblies (sometimes also called "councils," "courts," or "governing bodies"). We stated above that "since the whole church cannot meet together at one time and place to deliberate, representative governing bodies must be established on the various levels." Given that church power does not originate with the people, it is incorrect to say that people are represented in these assemblies. Rather, in those assemblies, the office-bearers represent Christ and govern on the people's behalf.

Nor is it accurate to say that each greater assembly represents the next lesser assembly. So we do not say that the classis represents the churches, nor the regional synod the classes, nor the General Synod the

16 Janssen, *Constitutional Theology*, 66.

17 Paul M. Fries, "Faithful Consistories," 281. In *MGS* 2000, 280–95.

18 *BCO*, Preamble, 3.

regional synods. And we most certainly cannot say that each of these assemblies represents confessing members, which people occasionally claim, as if the more populated areas of the church have a right of greater influence because of their greater numbers. However, there is an aspect of the current government of the Reformed church that is entirely out of step with the principle of representation: proportional delegation.

For most of the history of the Reformed church, the delegation to assemblies was equal. Between 1571 (the Synod of Emden) and 1874, the churches sent the same number of delegates to the assemblies, irrespective of the size of each church. The Church Order of Dort (1619) directed each church to send one minister and one elder to the classical assembly, two ministers and two elders were to be delegated to the particular synod, and two ministers and two elders from each of the particular synods to the General Synod.[19] It is certainly true that the affected churches were of different sizes, e.g., city churches would have been larger than country churches. Yet, because it is not the people but Christ who is represented, this delegation structure was entirely consistent with the church's theology of representation. In the RCA, a significant change happened in 1874 when the concept of proportional delegation was introduced for the General Synod in the course of a major revision of the church order. It is important to note that the Synod only applied it to the *number of churches* rather than to the number of members.[20] This still made theological sense because it treated the local church as the basic unit of the denomination. In 1909, however, the General Synod approved an amendment to the church order to apportion delegates to General Synod based on the number of (then-termed) communicant members on the rolls of the churches of each classis. The amendment was given no theological justification at the time. Later comments probably capture the actual reasoning: "it might fairly be maintained that this shift followed the cultural trend toward democratization in political life and the expansion of the franchise."[21]

The introduction of proportional delegation, especially by membership numbers, introduced a significant confusion into the church order and is not consistent with the church's historical understanding of representation. Despite this inconsistency, our church order still maintains that the assemblies do not represent constituencies. The basic unit of governance is the local church (consistory) and not individual confessing members, for truly the only constituency is the church of Jesus Christ.

19 Church Order of Dort, 1619, Arts. XLI, XLVII, L in Corwin, *Digest*.

20 Constitution, 1874, Art. 70 in Corwin, *Digest*.

21 *MGS* 2014, 236.

Not a hierarchy

The Reformed Church is not a hierarchy, not even a collegial hierarchy. It is plausible to imagine that the General Synod sits atop the Reformed Church and is "in charge" of the church, but this is not, in fact, true in our denomination. Not only is the General Synod not the supreme governing body of the church, but the authority of all the various assemblies is also tightly restricted and (mostly) delineated in the church order. Only the classis has a catch-all clause.[22]

As quoted previously, "Reformed governance understands the greater assemblies care for the ministry that extends beyond the purview of the lesser assemblies without infringing upon the responsibilities of the lesser." This understanding descends from a principle that has been present in every church order since Emden in 1571: for the synods, both provincial and general, nothing could be addressed other than those things which "could not be completed" in the lesser assemblies, or that "concern and affect all the churches."[23] And from here, we can see that the Reformed church intended to limit the greater assemblies, not allowing them to handle every matter, but only those matters that are too big for a lesser assembly or those that "concern and affect all the churches." Therefore, the ruling principle is that matters are to be handled as locally as is possible and proper.[24]

Ordinarily, then, the classis does not concern itself with the matters of the local church: that is the local consistory's responsibility. The classis, the regional synod, and the General Synod handle only matters pertaining to their respective purviews. The picture of our denomination's structure as a pyramid with the General Synod at the top and the local churches at the bottom, therefore, is not only a very inaccurate image, it is the image of a structure that we want to avoid. The responsibilities given to the various assemblies are responsibilities that shall be carried out and are not mere options. For instance, a classis is not allowed to avoid making a decision about superseding a consistory by asking the regional synod to decide instead. Responsibilities of the assemblies cannot be transferred to others.

The relations of the assemblies to one another indicate this flow of authority. The classis "shall report annually to the regional synod and

22 *BCO*, 1.II.2.11.

23 Acta of the Synod of Emden, 1571, Chapter III, Art. 1 and chapter IV. https://www.churchpolity.org/s/Acta-of-the-Synod-of-Emden-1571.pdf. Accessed 20 April 2021

24 Koffeman, *In Order to Serve*, 57, Plaatjies van Huffel, "The Relevance of Reformed Church Polity Principles," 39–40.

the General Synod upon the state of religion within the bounds of the classis."[25] This establishes the responsibility of each classis simply to inform the synods of the state of religion. Further,

> The classis shall report annually to the regional synod the names of persons who have been examined and licensed or ordained, all admissions and dismissions of ministers, all changes of pastoral relations, and the deaths of ministers within its bounds since the last session of the regional synod.[26]

The regional synod's role in the matter is only to record the information from the classis. The regional synod has no role in approving or disapproving any of these matters. The classis reports the information; the regional synod simply receives it. And finally, the classis annually appoints delegates to the synods, and the synods have absolutely no say in how a classis chooses delegates or whom they send. As long as the classis is acting in accordance with the church order, the synod's only action is to receive the credentials of the delegates and seat them.[27] The same actions pertain to the regional synod's relation with the General Synod. The regional synod reports on the state of religion within its bounds and appoints a delegate to the General Synod.[28] There is a permissive clause "the General Synod may assist the regional synods in the fulfillment of the common tasks of mission and ministry...." This, then, is something that the General Synod may do, but is not required to do. But even here, the order safeguards the integrity of the regional synods by adding, "...provided that such assistance does not infringe upon the prerogatives of the regional synods."[29] In the entire structure, the flow of relations moves from lesser to greater, rather than from the top downward.

It is, therefore, much more accurate to envision the denominational structure as concentric circles, where each circle is its own sphere of responsibility and authority and, ordinarily, a broader circle cannot invade the into the sphere of a smaller circle (See Figure 1).[30] "The idea that a

25 *BCO*, 1.II.19.1.
26 *BCO*, 1.II.19.2.
27 *BCO*, 1.II.19.3.
28 *BCO*, 1.III.7.1, 3.
29 *BCO*, 1.III.7.2.
30 It is important to note a distinction in language. The classis has both original and appellate supervisory power (BCO, 1.II.2.3), which means a case can be appealed to the classis, and a matter can originate in the classis. The synods, however, only have appellate supervisory power (BCO, 1.III.2.2; 1.IV.2.2), which means that matters

classis or synod could impose anything on a congregation is completely un-Reformed and of Roman Catholic origin."[31]

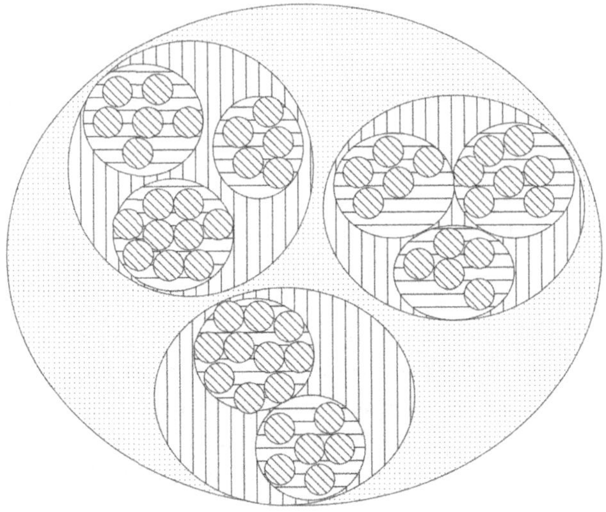

Figure 1

As the Commission on History worded it in a paper entitled, "A Historical Examination of the Relationship Among RCA Assemblies," the designed purpose of the greater assemblies "was not hierarchical, but conversational."[32]

One significant result of this principle is that the RCA does not grant magisterial authority to the General Synod, which is similar to the structures of many other Reformed churches.[33] Magisterial authority is the ability to give authoritative interpretations of the Scriptures, that is, to be the teacher of the church. If the General Synod were sitting at the "top," it might be consistent for a General Synod in that position also to have authority to give definitive and binding interpretations of Scripture or authoritative teachings of the faith. Given the structure of governance in the RCA, however, it would be entirely inconsistent for any such magisterial functions to be vested there or in any assembly at all, whether the General Synod or otherwise.

from the lesser assemblies, if they are to be handled in the synods, can only be done on an appeal, but matters concerning the lesser assemblies cannot originate in the synods.

31 Vos, *Reformed Dogmatics*, 5:73.

32 *MGS* 2007, 311.

33 Plaatjies van Huffel, "The Relevance of Reformed Church Polity Principles," 39.

That the General Synod does not have magisterial authority has been noted by the General Synod itself, perhaps most notably in the controversy over freemasonry, in which there was a strong push for the General Synod to ban membership in secret societies. The General Synod declined to do this, not because it had any fondness for secret societies (it even strongly discouraged participation), but rather because the General Synod was not permitted to take such an action.[34]

> The General Synod does not have among its powers the determination of what, finally, is the "teaching of the church." In Reformed church order, the teaching of the church is determined by the creeds and confessions of the church."[35]

Indeed, the work of interpreting and applying Scripture, and of interpreting and applying the creeds and confessions belongs not to the General Synod but is given to the bodies that have original authority over the situation in question—the board of elders in the case of a member, the classis in the case of a minister or a consistory. Further, not only are the synods not given that authority, it is impermissible for them to exercise authority that is not given to them. If an assembly takes on something that does not belong to it, it unfaithfully deprives the rightful body of the important work to which they have been called and ordained. This is something that both the greater and lesser assemblies must safeguard.

> A major meeting must also be vigilant not to take the actual functions of being church from the hands of the local congregation. Similarly, a local church council must always be vigilant not to want to transfer its authority to a major meeting.[36]

The representative principle is very important to understand how the church order works; however, it is equally important to properly understand who is being represented. Representation in the church is fundamentally different than representation in a liberal democracy, in that whereas, in a liberal democracy, the people are the ones who are, in the first place, represented; whereas in the church, Christ is the one who is, in the first place, represented. This has significant implications for how we understand the nature of the assemblies. The assemblies do not represent confessing members as it would if legitimacy was denied from the consent of the governed rather than from Christ. Related, the church is not a hierarchy,

34 *MGS* 1889, 839.
35 *MGS* 2005, 91.
36 Coertzen, *"Decently and in Order"*, 110.

and as such. The contrary, the authority of the greater assemblies is more circumscribed, and the authority of the lesser assemblies is broader.

CHAPTER 7

Governance by Elders

The Reformed churches have sought to follow the practice of the churches whose experience is recorded in the New Testament. The churches then were ruled by "presbyters" or "elders," just as the synagogues from which the first Christian converts came were ruled by elders. The Reformed churches consider the minister to be an elder of a special kind, called in some churches of the Reformed order, the "teaching elder." Ministers and elders therefore govern the church together. They also assist in the governing of the larger church by becoming from time to time members of the higher legislative assemblies or courts of the church. Thus also the lines of authority in the Reformed churches move from the local church to the General Synod. This is so since Christ, according to the New Testament, has appointed officers to govern the church under himself. Their authority to govern derives from him even though they are elected by the people. The local churches together delegate authority to classes and synods, and having done so, they also bind themselves to be subject together to these larger bodies in all matters

> in which the common interests of the many churches are objects of concern.
>
> While governance of the Reformed church is executed through the offices gathered in assemblies, the church expresses its full ministry through all its members in a variety of tasks. Each assembly is charged with determining the nature and extent of its ministry in faithful obedience to Scripture and in responsible concern for the church's mission in the world. Every member receives a ministry in baptism and is called with the whole church to embody Christ's intentions for the world.[1]

In the examination of this principle, we will examine the nature of governance and ministry, particularly the important role of the church members in the ministry of the church, even though they may not participate in the governance of the church. Finally, we will look at the flow of authority in the Reformed church.

Governance and ministry

Governance by elders is an inheritance from the ancient people of God.

> So the LORD said to Moses, "Gather for me seventy of the elders of Israel, whom you know to be the elders of the people and officers over them; bring them to the tent of meeting, and have them take their place there with you. I will come down and talk with you there; and I will take some of the spirit that is on you and put it on them; and they shall bear the burden of the people along with you so that you will not bear it all by yourself."[2]

One might even be able to say that "Israel's earliest memories portrayed her as a presbyterial people."[3] The monarchy disrupted this presbyterial structure, but after "the removal of the monarchy and its forceful centralizing pressure, elders re-emerge as the natural authorities at the local level."[4] As the early church emerged, it adapted many structures from the synagogue. For instance, Paul instructed Titus to "appoint elders in

1 Preamble, 4.

2 Num 11:16–17, NRSV.

3 James Tunstead Burtchaell, *From Synagogue to Church: Public Services and Offices in the Earliest Christian Communities*. (Cambridge: Cambridge University Press, 1992), 228. Presbyterial, that is, they were governed by elders.

4 Burtchaell, *From Synagogue to Church*, 229.

every town"[5] and that "elders who rule well" should "be considered worthy of double honor."[6] The Reformed, particularly in the Swiss regions, saw themselves as continuing this ancient and biblically-mandated tradition of governance by elders. As noted previously, the sixteenth-century reformation was not prompted by a single doctrinal point, as is sometimes suggested, but by a wide-ranging review of the foundations on which the prevailing social and religious systems were built. And in Switzerland, for instance, they needed to remake church and civil authority to replace the extensive powers of the pope and bishops. In this remaking, they appointed elders to handle disciplinary matters in the church and civil authorities to handle social order.[7] Their structures were not so clearly delineated as this description might connote, but this division shows us the general idea.

In the Reformed tradition, elders are not religious professionals. This is important. As Janssen notes, governance by elders helps guard the church against becoming a cleritocracy, that is, a church ruled by the clergy,[8] but it does much more than that:

> The ordained elder is not one who has forsaken his worldly or secular calling in order to enter into the religious calling of the church; on the contrary, in his role as the representative of sanctification around the Lord's table, he also continues his life as a grocer, a farmer, a union member, or a manufacturer. In him, the sanctifying power of the body and blood of Christ is carried into every corner of the world and into every aspect of its activity.[9]

Because of their continued vocations in the world, elders represent the "sanctification of the whole life."[10] That elders are not religious professionals is not incidental but central to their ministry as elders. Further, this is why the Reformed order holds the office of the elder, not the minister, to be the central office in Reformed order.

The Preamble notes that the minister is considered "an elder of a special kind" and that some presbyterial traditions make a distinction between teaching elders and ruling elders (what we know as minister

5 Titus 1:5, NRSV.

6 1 Tim 5:17, NRSV.

7 See Eugene P. Heideman, *Reformed Bishops and Catholic Elders* (Grand Rapids, MI: Eerdmans, 1970), 116-22.

8 Janssen, *Constitutional Theology*, 27.

9 Heideman, *Reformed Bishops and Catholic Elders,* 124.

10 *MGS* 1980, 104.

and elder, respectively). This identity of the minister as a "special kind" of elder, then, is why the minister and the elders together constitute the Board of Elders.[11]

The question of the role of the elder came to the fore in the 1990s when what we have now as preaching elders[12] was first being considered. The Commission on Theology sought to articulate the distinction between these related offices.

> In general...Reformed theology understands that a crucial role of the elder is to participate in the *oversight* of the preaching of the Word, whereas the minister's role is the actual *preaching* of the Word itself. ... In this way, discernment and proclamation complement each other in the governance of the church by the Word of God.
>
> If elders were to preach, it must be recognized that this distinction of role would become somewhat blurred....Nevertheless, preaching elders must realize that when they enter the pulpit they relinquish their supervisory and discerning role and become subject to the discernment and supervision of their preaching by the board of elders.[13]

Far from giving ministers control of the church, our church order gives the elders oversight over the content of the proclamation. In many instances, it is much to the surprise of local elders that they have the role of ensuring that what the minister preaches and teaches is faithful to the Scriptures!

The office of elder originates in the congregation: that is, the elder is a member of the local church, is elected by the local church, is ordained and installed in the local church, and serves chiefly in the local church. But, because the special function of the elder is the ministry of oversight, the elders also participate in the greater assemblies just as the Ministers of Word and Sacrament do. In classes and synods, ministers and elders participate equally. The voice and vote of minister and elder carry equal weight there.

What about deacons?

Deacons certainly have full membership on the consistory equal with the elders, but this is the only assembly of which deacons are a member. As we will see in the next chapter, this has nothing to do with

11 *BCO*, 1.I.1.2.

12 For preaching elders, see BCO, 1.II.16.

13 *MGS* 1996, 395.

having more or less importance than elders, but everything to do with the function of the offices. That is, governance is the province of the elder. But, given that, one may wonder why deacons participate in the church's governance at the consistorial level.

In the Church Order of Dort (1619), the consistory was defined as "the Ministers and Elders."[14] While deacons were also a necessary office (i.e., a local church could not decide not to elect deacons), they were not a part of the consistory. This is why the Christian Reformed Church, for example, includes only minister(s) and elders on the consistory, while the council also includes the diaconate.[15] Similarly, in the Presbyterian tradition, the local church is governed by the session composed of the ruling elders and teaching elder(s)/pastor(s).[16]

The RCA, however, has always included diaconal membership in its consistories. The Church Order of Dort did allow for deacons to be "admitted as members of the Consistory" when they were in places "where the number of Elders is too small."[17] The Explanatory Articles of 1792 note that "the Deacons have always in America, where the congregations were at first very small...been joined with the Elders."[18] And this is how deacons entered church governance in the RCA.

It makes sense for deacons to serve on the consistory in many ways. As the local church is the central manifestation of the church, the consistory will frequently have to address diaconal concerns. Deacons need to contribute to conversations in the consistory that consider "the nature and extent of the congregation's ministry in obedience to Holy Scripture and in response to the needs of the local community and the world."[19] Furthermore, matters related to property and finance are also clearly of diaconal concern.[20]

Deacons, however, do not participate in the greater assemblies (classes and synods) because the classes and synods have the primary purposes of oversight and governance.[21] Explanatory Article 38 once told

14 Article 37 in Corwin, *Digest.*

15 CRC, *Church Order and Its Supplements*, 2019, Art. 35.

16 PCUSA, *Book of Order*, 2019-2021, G-3.0201. Contrary, however, to the continental Reformed tradition, the PCUSA allows for congregations to decide (by majority vote!) to not utilize the office of deacon (G-2.0202).

17 Church Order of Dort, 1619, Art. 38, in Corwin, *Digest.*

18 Explanatory Articles, 1792, Art. 27 in Corwin, *Digest.*

19 *BCO*, 1.I.2.1.

20 *BCO*, 1.I.2.13.

21 We should note here that the ecclesial role of the classis is not the same as that of the synods. Oversight (*episcopé*) is central to the life and functioning of the church. While the Reformed Church is not episcopal, in that we do

us that, in a classis,

> an immediate representation of all the churches within those limits is formed; and a power of regulating the common measures for promoting religion, preventing error, and preserving peace within such a district is lodged. [22]

Thus the classis oversees the local churches to ensure that they properly attend to the ministry. The main responsibilities of the classis (supervising local churches, organizing local churches, supervision candidates for licensure and ordination, and the supervision of ministers) as assigned by the *BCO* show that this continues to be the case. Further, since the synods "exercise a general superintendence" and "an appellate supervisory power,"[23] the synods exist primarily for governance. All of this, then, shows why deacons do not participate in the greater assemblies despite being members of the consistory: the ministry of the elder is oversight while the ministry of the deacon combines mercy, service, and outreach, a ministry most fully expressed and lived out in the local church.

The ministry of the people

It is true that there are people in the church called "ministers," and this particular title exists for a good reason. However, this can give the false impression that these people called "ministers" are the only ones engaged in ministry. This is not the case. The ministry of the church is given from Christ to the *One Church* and to its diversity of local manifestations and to all the people in them, rather than to an episcopal hierarchy. In the Order for Profession of Faith, we read,

> By the Holy Spirit all who believe and are baptized receive a ministry
> to witness to Jesus as Savior and Lord, and
> to love and serve those with whom they live and work.

not have bishops, we have vested the ministry of oversight in the classis, for "the classis, and the classis alone, fulfills the episcopal function and all that it entails." (MGS 2018, 268). The synods, by contrast, do exist for governance and for the good order of the church, but they do not "constitute its essence." (Janssen, *Constitutional Theology*, 215).

22 Explanatory Articles, 1792, Art. 38 in Corwin, *Digest*. While the Explanatory Articles have been long-since replaced, they can help us, particularly from a historical perspective, deepen our understanding, as well as historical progression.

23 *BCO*, 1.III.2.1–2; 1.IV.2.1–2.

> We are ambassadors for Christ,
> who reconciles and makes whole.
> We are the salt of the earth;
> we are the light of the world.[24]

This passage uses "ministry" to refer to roles of Christian service in the church and world. God calls all members of the local church to such ministry. Most of the ministry of the church is carried out by the members. For example, because the church exists for mission in the world, the people are its missionaries. This kind of ministry by the members is essential and not incidental to the nature of the church. The ministry of the members is what the offices seek to sustain, uphold, and guard. The offices of the church exist "to equip the saints for the work of ministry, for building up the body of Christ."[25] Indeed, ministry understood in its "broadest sense denotes the service to which the whole people of God is called, whether as individuals, as a local community, or as the universal Church."[26]

The Dutch theologian Hendrik Kraemer argued that the church has one universal ministry and that everyone in the church, whether an office-bearer or not, shares in this one ministry.

> The Church *is* Ministry (diakonia) and therefore ministry is incumbent on the Church as a whole and not only on a special and specialized body of people "set apart" for the ministry, we have strongly stressed "the ministry of the laity" as an *integral* part of the Church's life and service. *All* members of the ekklèsia have in principle the same calling, responsibility and dignity, have their part in the apostolic and ministerial nature and calling of the Church.[27]

Because of this, Kraemer argues, we must emphasize "the laity's full, responsible share in bringing the nature and calling of the Church to expression."[28]

Authority that flows out

The local church is the most *church* as it gathers around Word and sacrament. As we have stated, Christ delegates authority to the church.

24 In *Worship the Lord*, 42.
25 Ephesians 4:12, NRSV.
26 *BEM*, section on Ministry, §7.
27 Hendrik Kraemer, *A Theology of the Laity* (Philadelphia: Westminster Press, 1958), 160.
28 Kraemer, *A Theology of the Laity*, 160-1.

This is not just to an ethereal, disembodied church, but to the concrete *One Church* that finds its primary embodiment and expression in the local church. The local church is where the *One Church* tangibly, concretely, specifically, and most clearly expresses itself. But the various local churches are not separate, precisely because they *are* expressions of the *One Church*, and all their members are members of the *One Body* of Christ. Therefore, they can act together as a larger concrete expression of the *One Church*. In the RCA, they do this, among other ways, by delegating specified authority to classes and synods. This is not simply a practical matter but also a theological matter of being the *One Church* together, binding themselves together in practice just as they are already connected with each other in the body of Christ. In other words, while the local church is wholly church, it is not the whole church. And by living in tangible and responsible relationships with other local churches, they express the *One Church* together. To understand how the RCA works both theologically and practically, we must understand this flow of authority. This flow embodies the RCA's understanding of the church and how the church order works and fits together (see Figure 2).

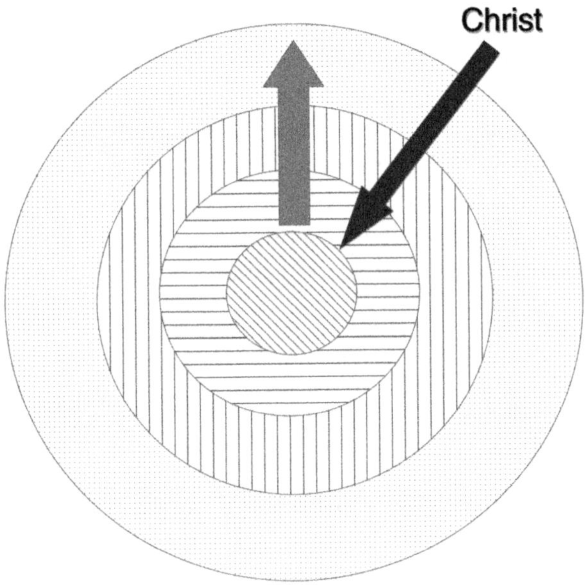

Figure 2

Christ delegates authority to the church, and the local churches "together delegate authority to classes and synods," thereby "also bind[ing] themselves to be subject together to these larger bodies in all matters in which the common interests of the many churches are objects of concern."

We derive this order from earlier church orders: e.g., we read in the Church Order of Dort,

> that which is decided by majority vote shall be considered settled and binding unless it is proved to conflict with the Word of God or with the articles adopted in this general synod as long as these are not changed by another general synod.[29]

The phrase "settled and binding" is strong but not absolute. First, "the Holy Scriptures are the only rule of faith and practice in the Reformed Church in America."[30] Consequently, all the decisions of any assembly are subordinate to Holy Scripture. The difficulty is that the RCA has no definitive interpretation of Scripture nor an independent magisterium to which such questions can be addressed. The question is whether this is a bug or a feature. I tend to think that it is a feature.

Second, the Dortian clause, "or with the articles adopted in this general synod," further means that the church order also regulates the activity of the assemblies. While the current church order does not use exactly the same words, it does note that all matters considered by the General Synod are to be matters of common concern of the churches, which takes us back to the discussion of the nature of the church's authority in chapter 2. This is yet another reminder that the power of the assemblies, especially the synods, to decide on matters is limited.

The elder is an inheritance from the ancient people of God. It is the elder, rather than the minister, that is the central office in Reformed order. Because they maintain a vocation in the world, elders represent the sanctification of the whole life. Elders help protect the church from becoming a cleritocracy, a rule by the clergy. Governance by elders continues through all of the assemblies, where elders and ministers have equal voice in the greater assemblies. Governance by elders, however, does not mean that the elders have a monopoly on the ministry of the church, for the members of the church are the ones charged with carrying out the ministry of the church. Finally, consistent with the principles of presbyterial order, authority does not flow down to the local church, but out the greater assemblies. Christ delegates authority to the church, which is most fully embodied in the local church, and some authority is further delegated to the greater assemblies.

29 Church Order of Dort, 1619, Art. 31, in Corwin, *Digest*.
30 *BCO*, Preamble, 1.

CHAPTER 8

Equality of the Ministry

> The Reformed Church in America uses the term "parity" to describe its concept of the equality of ministers. It is not meant that authority can never be exercised by one over the other. But in every instance this authority will be delegated by the proper body, and the authority will cease to be exercised when the need for it is no longer demanded. The principle of equality pertains also among churches, among elders, and among deacons. The principle of the equality of the ministry, conceived now in its broadest sense as including the functions of the elder and the deacon, is based upon the fact that the entire ministerial or pastoral office is summed up in Jesus Christ himself in such a way that he is, in a sense, the only one holding that office. Every ministerial function is found preeminently in him. By his Holy Spirit he distributes these functions among those whom he calls to serve in his name.[1]

This final principle is last, not because it is of the lowest rank, but because the linear nature of writing means that we can only present one

1 *BCO*, Preamble, 4–5.

matter at a time. This principle was one of the more revolutionary aspects of the sixteenth-century Reform movement, eliminating the three-dimensional structure of the church hierarchy with its bishops and cathedrals. Since Christ is the only head of the church, there is no head of the church nor a personal vicar of Christ on earth. As such, there is no person other than Christ himself from whom earthly church authority derives, and thus there is no need for a rank of clergy. To understand the importance of the equality of the ministry, we have to see it against the context of the hierarchical structures of the sixteenth century, especially in the context of their abuses. As the Reformed sought to go back to the sources and strip away the unnecessary baggage that had been added to the church, they arrived at the assertion of the Belgic Confession that teaches,

> As for the ministers of the Word, they all have the same power and authority, no matter where they may be, since they are all servants of Jesus Christ, the only universal bishop, and the only head of the church.[2]

The French Confession of 1559, one of the parent confessions of the Belgic, reads almost the same, though it also explicitly mentions the equality amongst churches. We see this equality amongst ministers reflected in the *BCO*, as well, "Ministers of Word and Sacrament are equal in authority as ministers and as stewards of the mysteries of God."[3]

Recognizing that Christ is the only head of the church has also led to the leveling of the church structure. Because office-bearers are accountable primarily to Christ and not to an episcopal hierarchy, all office-bearers have equal status, for they are all servants of Christ. This is also true for churches: because Christ delegates authority similarly to all churches and not to a hierarchy, there is no rank of churches, for all have equal power and status delegated to them by Christ. Whether a church is in the city or the country, big or small, collegiate or little chapel in the mountains, each and every one of these are understood to be of equal standing, equal importance, and equal dignity and authority with the others. This also reflects the church's governance as a christocracy rather than a democracy. If it were a democracy, churches with larger membership would be more important than smaller ones. The church, however, reflects the values of Christ's body and not the secular values that underlie liberal democracy.

2 Belgic Confession, Art. 31.

3 *BCO*, 1.I.1.3.

Since Christ is the universal bishop, there is no room to elevate any minister above others, as was done with medieval bishops. This means that we have no clerical class essentially different from the laity, but also no separate classes within the ministry that are higher than others. No one pledges obedience to a superior member of the clergy, as happens in a hierarchy.

The classis, in its function and status, results from the Reformed rejection of hierarchy. The Reformed also rejected the Lutheran arrangements to have superintendents replace bishops, which seemed too close to the Roman Catholic bishops.[4] This, of course, presented the Reformed Church with the problem of how to carry on oversight (the root of the word "bishop") without vesting the function in a personal bishop or superintendent. Our solution, remembering that the New Testament description of presbyter ("elder") included the function of overseer ("bishop") as well, was to establish oversight by a body of office-bearers. This not only reflects the Belgic Confession's insistence on the equality of ministers (since all offices reflect the ministry of Christ, and all ministry finds its origin and completion in Christ), but also the French *Ecclesiastical Discipline* of 1559 and repeated in the first article of the Synod of Emden in 1571:

> No church shall lord it over another church, no minister of the Word, elder or deacon shall lord it over another, but each shall guard himself against all suspicion and enticement to lord it over [others].[5]

This did not merely oppose a particular type of hierarchy, but all hierarchy.

We have dealt with this principle in the RCA when allowing elders to be commissioned as preaching elders. This commissioning does not make them some super-elder. Maintaining the equality of office was also one of the biggest challenges in defining the role of commissioned pastor. Commissioned pastors are elders who work in the circumstances very similar to those of a minister, so they might very easily be seen as a "higher" kind of elder or a "lower" kind of minister, which would, of course, violate this foundational principle of the equality of the ministry.

Just as there is no hierarchy within a given office, there is no hierarchy amongst the various offices. Although it is a frequent and unfortunate misconception, a deacon elected to become an elder is not being promoted.

4 Leon van den Broeke, "The History of the Classis," in Allan J. Janssen and Leon van den Broeke, eds. *A Collegial Bishop? Classis and Presbytery at Issue*. Historical Series of the Reformed Church in America, no. 66 (Grand Rapids, MI: Eerdmans, 2010), 11-12.

5 Acta of the Synod of Emden, 1571, Chapter I, Art. 1. https://www.churchpolity.org/s/Acta-of-the-Synod-of-Emden-1571.pdf. Accessed 20 April 2021

It is not uncommon for younger people to be elected deacon and, after a term or two, to be put forward as candidates for the office of elder. This treats deacons as junior elders or elders-in-training and degrades the office of deacon, treating it as a less important ministry of the church or even as an afterthought. On the contrary, the diaconal ministry is different, calling for gifts different from those of the elder and just as indispensable to the church. The deacon is seen as a lower office because they do not participate in the greater assemblies or handle matters of governance and discipline as the elders are called to do. Deacons handle material and physical matters, often seen as less important than governance. But they aren't.

No one office is higher or lower than another, no one office is more important than another, and no office is a minor office to the church. Although the Church Order of Dort (1619) did not put deacons on the consistory, this did not mean that deacons could be omitted. The diaconate has always been an essential office to the church. We see this reflected in the Liturgy,

> As the three offices of deacon, elder, and minister of Word and
> sacrament,
> are united in Christ,
> so also in the church one office is not separate from the others.
> The minister of Word and sacrament does not serve without
> the elder and neither without the deacon.
> Together they enable the whole mission of the church.
> Everything in the church will be done decently and in order
> when faithful persons are called to office and responsibly fulfil
> their charge.[6]

The church order itself is quite clear that "elders and deacons have an equal voice"[7] in the transaction of business on the consistory.

Because they are governing offices, ministers and elders constitute the same number of delegates from each classis at General Synod in an attempt to gain a minister/elder balance[8] for the voice, and the vote of a minister and an elder are in equal weight.

The misperception that our offices do have some kind of rank (e.g., ministers above elders above deacons) by power and importance is in part a result of confusing equality of importance with sameness. Governance

6 "Order for the Ordination and Installation of Elders and Deacons" in *Worship the Lord*, 46.

7 *BCO*, 1.I.4.1.

8 *BCO*, 1.IV.1.

is not more important than service, and participation in other bodies (which largely means going to more meetings) does not say anything about importance. Instead, in 1 Corinthians, St. Paul writes about the importance and necessity of all the gifts:

> The eye cannot say to the hand, 'I have no need of you', nor again the head to the feet, 'I have no need of you.' On the contrary, the members of the body that seem to be weaker are indispensable, and those members of the body that we think less honorable we clothe with greater honor, and our less respectable members are treated with greater respect; whereas our more respectable members do not need this. But God has so arranged the body, giving the greater honor to the inferior member, that there may be no dissension within the body, but the members may have the same care for one another.[9]

The refusal of the church to allow one group of people to control or domineer or exercise power over others should itself be one of the shining characteristics of the Church and every local church.

> You know that the rulers of the Gentiles lord it over them, and their great ones are tyrants over them. It will not be so among you; but whoever wishes to be great among you must be your servant, and whoever wishes to be first among you must be your slave; just as the Son of Man came not to be served but to serve, and to give his life a ransom for many.[10]

It is for this reason that we read, in 1 Peter, "Do not lord it over those in your charge, but be examples to the flock."[11]

Within the application of this principle, people do exercise positions of leadership and authority. Assemblies have presidents, persons who occupy a leadership position different from the others. Even here, however, as the Preamble notes, "But in every instance this authority will be delegated by the proper body, and the authority will cease to be exercised when the need for it is no longer demanded." Earlier generations put regulations into place that showed this more clearly. The Church Order of Dort, for example, notes that "The office of President shall cease when the Assembly rises [adjourns]."[12] While the minister was (and is) always

9 1 Cor 12:21-26, NRSV.
10 Matt 20:25b-28, NRSV.
11 1 Pet 5:3, NRSV.
12 Church Order of Dort, 1619, Art. 35 in Corwin, *Digest.*

the president of the consistory, the Church Order of Dort states, "if there be a plurality of Ministers, they shall preside and direct in rotation."[13] That order similarly requires that the same person is not to be "chosen twice successively"[14] as the president of the classical assembly. These regulations were all designed to guard against putting a bishop-in-all-but-name over others, as might happen the synod elected a president whose office existed all the time and had functions between the meetings of the assembly.

Our current church order does not have the same strict protections against the rise of a role similar to that of the medieval bishops, likely because of our distance from the problems that sparked the sixteenth-century reform movement. We can still nevertheless see that our assemblies do not treat the presidency as a position of power, but rather as a role that exists to "state and explain the business to be transacted, to enforce the rules of order, and in general, to maintain the decorum and dignity belonging to the church of Jesus Christ."[15] In some instances, the assembly can give the president additional tasks and responsibilities, but this is subject to the assembly itself. The president does not have any power over the assembly.

Even in these limited cases, any authority that a president may have rests with the *position* of the presiding officer and not with the individual *person*. Therefore, when the term of the presidency ends, so does all the authority vested in that position. This differs from some episcopal structures where the ordination of a person to become bishop thereby vests the person with certain powers that can be exercised in perpetuity.

The equality of the ministry is a foundational principle of presbyterial order. All offices are equally essential to the church's life, and within the offices, there are no degrees or ranks. The egalitarian nature of the church arises from the fact that Christ is the only head of the church, and therefore, not only is there no need for a hierarchy, such would be inappropriate. At times some can indeed exercise a particular authority that not everyone exercises; however, this authority is always temporary, never vested, and ceases when the role ceases.

13 Church Order of Dort, 1619, Art. 37 in Corwin, *Digest*.

14 Church Order of Dort, 1619, Art. 41 in Corwin, *Digest*.

15 *BCO*, 1.I.2.1; 1.II.5.1; 1.III.5.1; 1.IV.5.1.

EPILOGUE

By examining the foundational principles which underlie the presbyterial form of church polity, this book sought to provide a foundation for understanding the rhyme and reason of the order. Because the church order is not theologically neutral, it is important to understand the regulations from a legal perspective and a theological one. If we do not view the church order as a theological source, we will miss the entire point.

The Preamble begins with a strong declaration about the purpose of this entire enterprise.

> The purpose of the Reformed Church in America, together with all other churches of Christ, is to minister to the total life of all people by preaching, teaching, and proclamation of the gospel of Jesus Christ, the Son of God, and by all Christian good works. That purpose is achieved most effectively when good order and proper discipline are maintained by means of certain offices, governmental agencies, and theological and liturgical standards.[1]

1 *BCO*, Preamble, 1.

The church exists to bear witness to Jesus Christ holistically by proclamation of the gospel in word and deed. The church order does not exist to inhibit this work but to facilitate it. The order exists for the sake of the church; the church does not exist for the sake of the order. This does not mean that we treat the church order as optional and that we can set it aside when it is most convenient to do so.

And finally, the one important unwritten thread that holds everything together: trust. Trust in Christ to continue to guide and uphold the church, the trust that Christ, through Word and Spirit, continues to govern Christ's church; trust that the office-bearers and assemblies are seeking to listen to Christ through Word and Spirit and be obedient to Christ as the only head of the church. This does not mean that we will always agree, but we need this basic level of trust. Too often, when things turn out the way we prefer, then we have listened to Christ. But if things have not turned out the way we wished, we have ignored Christ. This is not to say that every view is equally valid, but we cannot assume that Christ is only present when things turn out the way we wish.

A church order is not something that can hold a church together. Christ is the One who holds a church together; we cannot look to a church order to do the heavy lifting of this essential work. We can only look to the One who called us, the One who redeemed us, the One who continues to uphold us. Indeed, Christ is the only One to whom we can look.

APPENDIX 1

Glossary

Assembly – A governing body in the Reformed Church composed of office-bearers, especially ministers and elders. The four assemblies in the Reformed Church are the Consistory, the Classis, the Regional Synod, and the General Synod.

Book of Church Order – This book contains (1) the Preamble, (2) the Government, (3) the Disciplinary and Judicial Procedures, (4) the Formularies, and (5) the Bylaws and Special Rules of Order of the General Synod. All but the number five are part of the constitution.

Christocracy – Rule by Christ. Understanding Christ as the only head of the church makes the church a christocracy rather than a democracy or a monarchy.

Church order – A code of regulations that helps to order and regulate the life and ministry of a particular church or denomination. In most cases, in this text, the stand-alone term "church order" relates to the *Book of Church Order* of the Reformed Church in America.

Church polity – The discipline that studies the regulations that govern churches from a theological perspective. Church polity, then, is a discipline or field of study. At the same time, a church order is a specific application of this field to the life and ministry of a particular church/ denomination.

Classis – A Latin term referring to a fleet of ships. The classis consists of all the ministers within its bounds and elder delegates from the various churches within its bounds. The classis exercises oversight over the consistories and ministers within its bounds, and as such, exercises the episcopal (oversight) function in the Reformed Church. (plural: classes)

Congregational – A church organization in which authority is lodged in the congregation. A congregational church polity generally leans democratic in orientation.

Consistory – The most local assembly in the Reformed church and the governing body for the local church. The consistory is composed of the elders and deacons elected by the congregation and the minister(s) serving under a call. The consistory is further subdivided into the two constituent boards: Board of Elders and Board of Deacons.

Constitution – A document that constitutes a body. A constitution does not include everything, nor all the important things, but those things that are constitutive. In most cases, the term "constitution" in this text refers to the Constitution of the Reformed Church in America. The RCA's Constitution includes the Government with the Disciplinary and Judicial Procedures, the Liturgy with the Directory for Worship, and the Doctrinal Standards.

Deacon – An ordained ministry "set apart for a ministry of mercy, service, and outreach" (1.I.1.8). A congregation elects them to serve on its consistory. The deacons serving on consistory constitute the Board of Deacons.

Delegate – Both a verb and a noun are spelled the same. As a verb, to delegate is to grant someone(s) the ability to act on their behalf. As a noun, a delegate is granted the ability to exercise authority on behalf of another. Elders are delegated to classical assemblies, and ministers and elders are delegated to synodical assemblies.

Doctrine or **Doctrinal Standards** – The official teaching of the Reformed Church. This consists of the Belgic Confession with the Canons of Dort, the Heidelberg Catechism with its Compendium, and the Belhar Confession.

Ecclesiology – The field of theology that focuses on the study of the church.

Elder – An ordained ministry "set apart for a ministry of watchful and responsible care for all matters relating to the welfare and good order of the church" (1.1.1.6). A local church elects elders to serve on its consistory. The elders serving on consistory with the minister(s) form the Board of Elders. From time to time, elders are delegated to classical and synodical assemblies.

Episcopal – A structure of governance that utilizes bishops to perform oversight (*episcopé*). Episcopal church polities are often, but not always, hierarchical. Episcopal polity generally leans monarchical in orientation.

Greater assemblies – Assemblies with increasing breadth of scope. Classis, Regional Synod, General Synod may be referred to as "greater," particularly in that order. This term carries no significance regarding importance, power, or authority.

Hierarchy – A structure of organization where different levels are ranked above one another by authority. A hierarchy may be described as a "top-down" structure.

Lesser Assemblies – Assemblies with a smaller or narrower scope. Regional Synod, Classis, and Consistory may be called lesser assemblies in that order. This term carries no significance regarding importance, power, or authority.

Liturgy – The Liturgy is a part of the Constitution of the Reformed Church. This was historically divided into obligatory forms (Lord's Supper, Baptism, Profession of Faith, Ordination, Installation, and Discipline) and optional forms, which are everything else. This historic division shows the distinction between the Liturgy (constitutional) and liturgies (not constitutional).

Magisterial authority – the ability to give an authoritative and binding interpretation of the scriptures or a point of doctrine. The magisterium, the teacher of the church, is the Doctrinal Standards, and the synods are not empowered to make interpretations that are binding on all the churches and assemblies.

Minister of Word and Sacrament – An ordained ministry in the church "called to proclaim the gospel of Jesus Christ and to the ministry of the Word of God" and to administer the sacraments (1.I.1.4). Ministers can serve as a pastor and teacher of a local church or serve in a classis-approved specialized ministry. Ministers are ordained by, under the supervision of, and members of the classis.

Office – An ordained ministry within the church. Offices are ministries "servanthood and service representing Christ through the action of the Holy Spirit." Essential to being ordained to an office is a call by God and by a particular congregation for a specific ministry. The four offices in the RCA are Minister of Word and Sacrament, Elder, Deacon, and General Synod Professor. All offices represent a facet of Christ's ministry.

Presbyterial – Governance by elders (presbyters). This form of governance lodges governing authority in a body of elders rather than a bishop or the congregation as a whole. The Reformed Church is governed according to the presbyterial order.

Synod – From the Greek words *syn,* which means with and *odos,* which means way, and can be translated as "together on the way." Synods are assemblies for governance that have appellate supervisory power in their area of responsibility. Synods are made up of minister and elder delegates from the classes. Synods are Regional or General.

APPENDIX 2

Discussion Guide

Chapter 1

- What does it mean that the RCA has a constitution, and why does it matter?
- What has been your experience with the different legs of the Constitution: Doctrine, Liturgy, and Government?
- How do the three modes impact the function of the three legs of the Constitution, and how have you seen these modes in practice?

Chapter 2

- How are the four attributes of the church present in the life of your local church, and why is this important?
- How are the three Reformation marks embodied in your local church?
- If the local church is the most *church*, then why is it important to be connected together with other churches?

Chapter 3

- Why does Christ being the only head of the church preclude the church from being either a monarchy or a democracy, and what is the significance of this for the life of the church?

Chapter 4

- How are the church offices understood in your local church?
- How are the three types of authority exercised in your local church?

Chapter 5

- Why is church membership important?
- If someone said to you, "church membership isn't in the Bible, and therefore we shouldn't practice it," how might you respond?
- How is church membership understood in your local church?

Chapter 6

- In what ways is representation in the church different from representation in a liberal democracy, and what does it matter?
- What is the difference between a democracy and a christocracy, and why does it matter?
- Concentric circles are better than a pyramid to diagram the structure of the RCA. Why is this so?

Chapter 7

- What is the significance of the church being governed by elders?
- How does governance by elders and the ministry of the people complement one another?
- What is the significance of authority flowing outward rather than inward/downward?

Chapter 8

- What does equality of the ministry mean?
- Are "equality" and "sameness" the same? Why or why not?
- Why is the equality of the ministry important?

APPENDIX 3

Hermeneutics of Church Polity

The church order is not a code of laws made wholly, or even chiefly, to efficiently carry out business and oversight; on the contrary, it is a thoroughly theological document. It continually points us to Christ and to the nature of the Church as the body of Christ, and seeks thereby to enable our church to understand and embody the true nature of the church in light of Scripture and our theological and confessional tradition. This means that the church order is not simply a code of laws that can be examined or even understood in isolation from that theology, nor is it merely a set of boxes to tick or regulations to work around however one can. Because church polity is a theological discipline, approaching the church order requires that one have some ability to interpret the church order, not only to interpret and apply the regulations themselves but more importantly to understand why the regulations are there and what purpose they serve. To live "in order" in the church requires this to apply the church order to real-life situations in a more faithful and Christ-oriented way. In short, we need to consider hermeneutics.

Hermeneutics is the field of study that deals with interpretation. Applying the church order requires at least a degree of interpretation.

Understanding the church order goes beyond knowing details of its requirements. Church order is like a handbook for operating the church. We can (and mostly do) drive automobiles with only a limited understanding of how the machine works. But those entrusted with the church's governance are more like auto mechanics, who are entrusted not only with driving and repairing the car but also occasionally re-writing the owner's manual. If we don't understand the nature of the machine entrusted to us, we are in danger of doing considerable damage to machine and passengers alike. The manual is not arbitrary. Understanding the church order is something that can be done! Like learning anything else, it takes study, effort, time, and experience.

Some elements of the order are relatively straightforward, for instance, "All consistory meetings shall include Scripture and shall begin and end with prayer."[1] This is quite clear and does not require much, if any, interpretation. Other occasions for using the church order, however, need careful and wise interpretation; for instance, "A classis has the authority, after trial, to suspend a consistory accused of unfaithfulness to duty, or of disobedience to the classis..."[2] In this case, what does "disobedience to the classis" mean? For instance, if the classis demanded that all of its churches paint their sanctuaries orange, could the classis try the consistory and suspend them from office for disobedience? This is an extreme and absurd example, but it illustrates the matter at hand: does the order empower a classis to demand anything and everything it likes from a local church, backed up with the absolute power of suspension?[3] Of course not. Discerning proper and orderly demands from a classis is one example of the necessity for wise interpretation, illustrating why we must give attention to the hermeneutics of church polity.

Because a church order is theological, we must read it as a theological document. As such, it must be read and understood as something that conforms to our understanding of God's desires for the church. We begin not from the question of whether something is efficient or easy; we begin with the affirmation that a faithful church order will reflect God's desires for the church. This starting point shapes every step that follows it. The reason for many rules in the church order may not be obvious at first glance: Why do we require the classis to approve calls to ministers? How does that reflect God's desires for the church? Part of the work of reading and using a church order is to ask questions like that and then look below

1 *BCO*, 1.I.4.3.

2 *BCO*, 2.I.3.6.

3 In short, the answer is no, the classis cannot demand anything.

the regulations themselves to the purpose, meaning, and value, looking backward at the principles behind the idea and forward at its results. Reading a church order in harmony with one's confessions and tradition helps illuminate our examinations. In our case, we read the church order alongside the Belgic Confession, the Canons of Dort, the Heidelberg Catechism, and the Belhar Confession first of all. In the second place, we also refer to the broader Reformed tradition, which includes these but expands beyond them—to say nothing of the broader Christian tradition with which church polity is in dialogue. If the Doctrinal Standards are the teachers of the church, which is their intended use, then we must also take instruction from them as we approach the church's governance. It is this larger theological framework that this book seeks to address and illuminate. Without examining the theological and historical foundations of our church order, we will not understand that order, and we thereby put ourselves in danger of misusing it.

Particular regulations must be read in their immediate context and the context of the church order as a whole. What are the regulations around it? What do these indicate, and might there be lessons gained from these which can be helpful for understanding and applying this particular regulation?

As noted above, a church order must be theologically accountable, and similarly, one has to look at the ecclesiology expressed in the regulation. What is at stake? What might be the theological value which underlies the regulation? By examining the regulation in light of these questions and questions like them, we can begin to gain a fuller understanding of the regulation and its reason for being there (and in some cases, also why it should be changed).

Regulations often also have complicated and illuminating histories and backgrounds. I often tell my students that the regulations in the church order are answers to concrete, particular questions. They did not fall from heaven, nor did people sit in a room and think them up out of thin air. Every one of the regulations was born from a real and practical—and at the time, very alive—question that the church was facing. We cannot understand the regulations apart from these questions. When we can discover the questions they were asking, we can begin to gain more insight into the intention of the regulation and the values and concerns that are at stake. The "References to the *Minutes of General Synod*" in the back of the *BCO* is very valuable to this end. By tracing the history of a regulation back through history, we can gain some insight into its purpose and why it was changed.

Further, almost every regulation also has a history that dates before the references given in that section. For instance, the principle of the equality of the ministry is a very old principle that goes back to the very first generation of the sixteenth-century Protestant Reformation. Therefore we look also at the backdrop against which it was articulated and the historical and social milieu out of which it came. Even when we do not have a specific document saying, "we did this because…," how the regulation operated in the past can be instructive about its purpose. This is one of the areas where the work of church historians, particularly historians of church polity, are especially valuable so that we do not each have to reinvent the wheel each time we are wondering about a particular regulation.

Excursus: Special Session of the General Synod[4]

An example may shed some light on the practice of church polity hermeneutics. Whether or not we agree with the actions that took place is not the point. The goal here is to use an event in our recent past to show how we can use various tools to understand not only the words or our church order but also the meaning.

In 2020, during the COVID-19 pandemic, the General Synod Council (GSC) acted as an executive committee of the General Synod when it voted to cancel the 2020 session of the General Synod and call a special session in October of that year. There is a separate but related question of whether the GSC can (or should be able to) cancel sessions of the General Synod, but this is not the question we examine here. The urgency for the General Synod to meet in some form in 2020 largely arose because the Vision 2020 Task Force had completed its deliberations and report. The denomination needed a way of handling their recommendations.

The regulation governing the calling of special sessions of the General Synod reads as follows:

> The president of the General Synod shall call a special session of that synod at a place determined by the president, vice president and the general secretary of the synod upon the joint application of three ministers and three elders from each of the regional synods, all of them serving currently as accredited delegates to the General Synod.

4 This appeared previously in essentially the same form at, Matthew van Maastricht, "Special Meetings of the General Synod," *Church and Order: Reflections in Protestant Church Polity* (blog). April 30, 2020, https://churchandorder.org/2020/04/30/special-meetings-of-the-general-synod/

> Three weeks' notice of the session shall be given to the members of the synod, such notice to state the purpose of the session.[5]

There is, however, no mention of the executive committee calling for a special session. The General Synod office reasoned that the above regulation only specifies when special sessions *must* be called but does not speak about other times in which a special session *may* be called. And because the New York State nonprofit corporation law allows for a board of directors to call a special session, the GSC did so under that authority. For the GSC to decide that they are permitted to call a special session whenever they decide they have a good reason for doing so requires a huge interpretive leap, particularly as it makes an argument from complete silence. This would make more sense if the church order generally only said what cannot happen, but it doesn't do that. In most instances, it says what *should* happen.

What is more, the background of this decision is not complete silence in the church order because other parts of the church order establish a pattern for similar situations. Regarding the consistory: "The president shall call special meetings of the consistory when they are deemed necessary and shall do so promptly when requested by at least three members of the consistory."[6] Furthermore, the classis: "The president of classis shall call a special session of classis whenever special business requires it or upon the written request of two classis members and two elder delegates."[7]

However, the language changes regarding calling special sessions of the synodical bodies. For the regional synod, "The president of the regional synod shall call a special session of the synod upon receipt of a written request of one minister and one elder delegate from each of the classes within its bounds."[8]

And finally, for the General Synod:

> The president of the General Synod shall call a special session of the synod at a place determined by the president, vice president and the general secretary of the synod upon the joint application of three ministers and three elders from each of the regional synods, all of them serving currently as accredited delegates to the General Synod.[9]

5 *BCO*, 1.IV.4.2.
6 *BCO*, 1.I.4.6.
7 *BCO*, 1.II.4.2.
8 *BCO*, 1.III.4.2.
9 *BCO*, 1.IV.4.2.

One may, of course, say that the language for the consistory or the classis does not matter here. However, reading the church order contextually and understanding that the church order is an integrated whole with a largely consistent logic, the relevance and value of the other parts become apparent. One may also say that the same latitude for the president to call a special session of the synods when it is "deemed necessary" or when "special business requires it" is implied because the church order allows it for the consistory and classis. So a consistent interpretation of the church order implies that the president of this assembly may call a special session, even though the church order does not specifically say so. One may also argue that the church order only specifies when a special session *must* be called but leaves open the matter of when one *may* be called. However, all of these arguments are, I think, tenuous at best, particularly when we look theologically and historically at this question.

Theological perspective

> Synods differ essentially from consistories or even classes:
>
> while the synods were necessary for the good order of the church, they did not constitute its essence. Reformed churches could— and did—exist without a national synod. Reformed people understood that *Christ* constituted his church through Word and Spirit. That happened as the living Word, Christ, called his people around pulpit and Table. The synods existed, then, as the *bene esse*, for the good of the church, but not as the *esse*, the essence of the church.[10]

A synod, then, is not just a bigger version of a classis or a consistory. To think of it as such is to misunderstand our church order. As we have said previously, the church is the most *church* when it gathers around pulpit, table, and font, and each broader ring around that local body is *church* in a more derivative form. The synods are bodies without permanent memberships. It is questionable how a synod can be *church* in any meaningful sense of the term when it is not an ongoing locus of Word and sacrament. [11]

10 Janssen, *Constitutional Theology*, 215–16.

11 This is the reason that minsters who are "installed as a pastor of a local church shall be a member of that church by virtue of installation," and that "A minister not installed as a pastor shall become a member of a local church" (BCO 1.II.15.6). Ministers are members of the classis, but they also have a (somewhat different but definite) membership in the local church. Practically speaking, this is a challenging or odd thing, but it recognizes the reality that ministers, too, live within the church as the church gathers around pulpit, table, and font.

Because of this difference in essence between the consistory and classis on the one hand, and the synods on the other, treating our church order responsibly excludes the option of easily glossing over the differences in the order. The matter should, at least, give us pause. Indeed, the order offers the possibility for "if needed" optional special sessions as well as when the requisite number from the body calls for them. I find it peculiar that our church order does not make similar provision for the synods since it explicitly does so for two assemblies and does not for two others. That difference should and does contribute to the wisdom necessary for interpreting our church order.

The language for the consistory, "when they are deemed necessary," is the broadest and most permissive wording. In a way, this makes great sense. Because of the innumerable number of things that a consistory must handle, it makes sense that a special session could be called whenever it is "deemed necessary."

The language for the classis is quite broad but a bit more restrictive, "whenever special business requires it." The word "requires" adds a sense of stricter need rather than desire or "deeming." The order does not specify what special business would have to be required, but earlier church orders indicate what type of business is in view.

> It shall be the duty of the president of the Classis to call its members together by circular letter when a special meeting of the Classis is made necessary for an examination, an approval of a call, an ordination, and installation, or any other special business."[12]

Here we can see the examples given are necessary things and things that the classis must do and that only the classis can do. These cannot wait for a stated session if they come between sessions. And the "any other special business" is narrowed through "necessary" and things that are similarly necessary to those given in the list.

We have two words here, "necessary" used previously and "required" used in the current church order. And so, while the order allows for special sessions to be called for apart from the requisite number of members/delegates to apply for one, it is still restricted by what is "required." However, when at least two ministers and two elders request a special session, one must be called, regardless of the reason. This allows the body to have control over special sessions, as well.

But when we get to the synods, we have neither the very broad discretion of the consistory nor the more limited discretion of the classis.

12 Constitution, 1916, Art VII, Sec. 91.

Still, we have the complete absence of any provision for discretionary special sessions. The church order only opens the possibility of special sessions when the requisite number of delegates call for them. Coincidentally (or intentionally), this reflects the distinction between the essence (*esse)* and the well-being (*bene esse)* of the assemblies. While some may argue that this is an oversight, it is an oversight that has existed since the General Synod started allowing special sessions in 1800. It is hard for me to believe that a difference in language that has existed this long and has persisted through so many revisions, even global revisions, of the church order is simply an oversight.

Furthermore, there is also the fact that the synods, and the General Synod particularly, draw delegates from a much greater geographic area with a greater variety of interests, concerns, views, and the like. It is easier for a president of a consistory to determine what is a desired matter for a special session, it is even easier for the president of a classis to determine when a special session is required, but it is very difficult for the president of a regional synod or the General Synod to determine what matters are (a) both necessary and (b) of a concern for the whole church. Indeed, this, I think, is why for the synods, the only provision in the church order for calling a special session is for the requisite number of delegates to apply for it.

> It would be a daunting and expensive task to gather a special session of a national body. Special circumstances, however, may require the synod to meet in an extraordinary session. The order recognizes the extraordinary nature of such sessions by constructing imposing conditions for their call. Three ministers and three elders from each synod would, at the present time, mean that at least 48 delegates request a special session. And since *each* synod must provide six signatures, the need would encompass the entire variety of the church's life. Thus no one theological or ecclesiastical commitment would be capable of engineering a special session.[13]

Historical perspective

In the latter half of the eighteenth century, when the newly independent Reformed Church was beginning its organization, special sessions of General Synod were not uncommon. The Explanatory Articles of 1792 allowed the General Synod to "make regulations from time to

[13] Janssen, *Constitutional Theology*, 229.

time, for calling an extraordinary session" (Art. 55). Each of the first two General Synods under the newly (at that time) adopted Constitution (1794 and 1797) determined the time it would once again convene and permitted the President to call a special session if needed between the triennial stated sessions.

In 1800, the General Synod passed a resolution,

> *Resolved*, That if circumstances should require a meeting of the General Synod previous to the next Ordinary Meeting, the President be, and he is hereby authorized, on a joint application of six or more ministers requesting the same, to call an Extraordinary meeting."[14]

This was the first time there was a standing rule for special sessions, and it is clear, even from the beginning, that the president alone is not authorized to call a special session but must receive an application of six or more ministers. This was codified into the church order of 1833 (Chapter II, Article V, Sec. 5).[15]

Even in extraordinary times, this joint application was required. The session of 1803, for instance, decided to adjourn to October. Meeting in October was not possible, and the synod reconvened in May 1804. At the beginning of the Acts of that special session, we read the introduction to the meeting,

> having been prevented by the interposition of Divine Providence for holding the session in October last, according to their adjournment at Poughkeepsie, a competent number of ministers concurred to request the President to call a meeting of Synod, and the present meeting was duly called...[16]

It did not take long for the requirements to call a special session to be altered from six ministers to six ministers *and* six elders. The church order of 1833 provided for special sessions,

> If circumstances should require a meeting of the General Synod previous to the next ordinary meeting, the President shall, on a joint application of six Ministers and six Elders requesting the same, call an extraordinary meeting..." [17]

14 *MGS* 1800, 312.
15 *MGS* Oct 1832, 127.
16 *MGS* May 1804, 322.
17 Constitution, 1833, Chapt 2, Art 4, Sec. 4, in Corwin *Digest*

The language deserves our close attention. "If circumstances should require..." addresses a contingency with its initial "if." If there is something that requires a special session, then the President shall call for one on a joint application with six ministers and six elders. The requirement provides no other way to call a special session apart from the joint application of the requisite number of elders and deacons. The language of this section of the church order remained virtually unchanged for decades: as the Reformed Church grew, so did the requisite number of people required for calling a special session. The requirement set at the beginning of the twentieth century for twelve ministers and twelve elders remained until 1960 when the current requirement of three ministers and three elders from each particular/regional synod who are currently serving as accredited delegates to the General Synod was incorporated into the order.

The matter of special sessions, then, has a fairly straightforward line from 1800 to today, even though there have been changes in the number of people involved and the requirement (1960) that they are from each particular synod and be accredited delegates to the General Synod.

David D. Demarest, however, regarded this provision in the church order as so clear that in his commentary, *Notes on the Constitution of the Reformed (Dutch) Church in America*, he writes, "An explanation of this section is not necessary."[18] David Demarest's son and the eminent Reformed Church polity teacher and commentator, William H.S. Demarest, who wrote a little green-covered volume of the same title as his father, did not offer much detail on the special sessions of General Synod, particularly because they had fallen into disuse by the time that he was writing,

> A special session of the General Synod is rarely called, has not been called in many years. It was held occasionally in the past years when the church was more compact, the synod much smaller, for the election of a theological professor.[19]

We should note that even these rare special sessions were typically called when the denomination needed to elect a theological professor. In the early generations, the General Synod elected *all* of the professors to the seminary. Therefore, when a professor resigned or died suddenly, the

[18] David D. Demarest, *Notes on the Constitution of the Reformed (Dutch) Church in America* (New Brunswick, N.J.: J. Heidingsfeld's Press, 1896), 137.

[19] William H.S. Demarest, *Notes on the Constitution of the Reformed Church in America* (New Brunswick, N.J.: New Brunswick Theological Seminary, 1928), 143.

seminary needed a replacement and could not wait until the next ordinary session, thus necessitating a special session.

In surveying several special sessions from the nineteenth century (a list which I will not claim to be exhaustive), I looked at nearly twenty special sessions,[20] of which a handful were adjourned sessions (when the General Synod, at its ordinary meeting, decided to reconvene at a later time). Of those that were not adjourned sessions, the majority were called to elect professors, and a minority handled matters like disciplinary problems. In terms of the method employed to call them, the adjourned sessions did not require any special method since the General Synod itself decided to do this. Of those that were not adjourned sessions, approximately three did not give indications as to the method of their calling. Still, the remainder began with some form of, "The President laid before the synod a constitutional request which he had received to call an extra meeting of the Synod." Here, we can see the phrase "constitutional request," which I cannot understand as anything but an application by the requisite number of elders and ministers as provided for in the Constitution.

Therefore, nearly every instance that I was able to find indicated that the special session was called in the method specified by the church order.

But what about the General Synod Council?

One difference between today's Reformed Church and the Reformed Church in the times of special sessions is the presence of an executive committee of the General Synod. The General Synod Council has argued that, because the New York non-profit corporation law allows the board of directors to call a special session, the General Synod Council is empowered to do so.[21] But this argument ignores the actions of the Reformed Church's board of directors in previous years. After the General Synod was incorporated in 1819, state law required that the church have one. The Board of Direction of the Corporation (though the name changed somewhat over the years) was the board of directors. In 1970, the then-separate Board of Direction was folded into the General Synod Executive Committee by replacing members of the Board of Direction with GSEC members when their terms expired.[22]

[20] 1804, 1815, Jan 1823, Feb 1823, 1825, 1826, 1828, 1831, 1832, 1840, Sept 1841, Oct 1841, 1849, 1855, 1857, 1867, 1871, 1881.

[21] This argument only works if we also assume that the General Synod Council derives its authority from the State of New York in this matter, not from the General Synod, and without regard to the relevant consideration of the *Book of Church Order*.

[22] *MGS* 1970, 183–84.

The actions taken by those boards, however, conformed to the requirements of the church order, that is, in almost every instance when a special session was not an adjourned session type special session, the requisite number made an application of ministers and elders to call such a session. The president never called one at his (and at the time, they were all "his") discretion, nor did the Board of Direction call one.

Why does this matter?

The General Synod has, as its charge, the interests and concerns of the whole church. A special session, then, falls within those same interests and concerns. Whether the special session in October was necessary is open to debate. Even so, however, it is not required. The conditions given for calling a special session serve as a bar, and a rather low one, to be honest, to determine whether it is a concern of the whole church or a special interest within the church. If a special session in October indeed was the concern of the whole church, then there should not be any problem with actually meeting the relatively low bar given in the order. Any concern that the requirements could not be met (and even the plausibility of that concern remains to be established), the question remains whether it is truly a matter of urgent concern of the whole church. Another way of looking at it is to respond that the GSC is not charged with determining whether requirements for a special session can be met, but only with organizing that session if they *are* met, and if not, then not.

The question is what is allowed and what is best for the church. Did the church at large want to discuss the report of the 2020 Task Force in a brief and focused and emotionally intense special session, in isolation from the other work of the church, seeing only a narrow and grossly incomplete view of the work and life of the church, and in a session that cannot amend (propose or adopt changes to) the Constitution or the Bylaws of the General Synod?[23] This is a question with which the church could and should wrestle. We do need, as a denomination, to address a narrow and a broad matter. The narrow matter is to specify more clearly how we shall cancel meetings of General Synod or call special sessions of General Synod in the future, and for what purposes. The broader matter is to specify what authority the General Synod Council does and does not have for acting in the absence of the General Synod.

[23] *BCO*, p. 75, sec 2a; 3.I.11.

Postscript

Between the time that this piece was written and when this book is published, the church is finding a way to navigate these questions. At the 2021 General Synod, a proposal was approved on first reading for a Committee on Emergencies. This proposal is a brilliant one that finds an excellent balance between practicality and principle. The proposal is a way to respond to the context in which we find ourselves and doing things decently and in good order, fitting in what we understand about the church.

It does not take much effort to imagine several plausible ways in which there would be a problem with the functioning of the General Synod at the appointed time and place. Perhaps it will be another pandemic. Perhaps it may be a tornado, fire, or flood. None of these are a stretch to imagine happening in real life. It is nothing short of a miracle that we have not encountered this problem before now.

The proposed Committee on Emergencies, "shall be convened whenever necessary in response to a disaster or crisis that would prevent the General Synod from meeting in its stated session or disrupt plans to hold a session at a particular venue, such as a fire, natural disaster, or another sudden calamity." It is to be made up of the General Synod President, Vice president, immediate Past President, and the General Secretary—all without a vote. The bulk of the proposed Committee is the presidents (or a president's designee) of all the classes. The proposal specifies specific and limited actions that this Committee would be permitted to take and the threshold of approval that is required to take any or all of those actions.

This proposed change to the Bylaws of General Synod allows for a creative solution to what currently presents something of an impasse. And it does so without sacrificing what we affirm about what we believe about the church.

Finally, this provides an example of the real reason that we study church polity. We study church polity not because we like rules, or want to prevent change, or stand in the way of things, but because we love the church and how we do things and why we do things is just as important as what we do. Because the church is made up of people who live in the world, very few things are predictable. More often than not in the life of the church, things come up for which there is no clear right answer. Sometimes our job is not to find the right answer, but to find the best out of many possibilities, or—as is often the case—the least bad option. We do this by finding the values that are expressed in the Constitution and trying to, as faithfully as we can, apply them to the situation at hand.

There are two levels when it comes to understanding the church order. The first level is knowledge. Knowing what is in the church order and knowing where to turn in the book for the answer. Knowledge can be gained fairly easily and quickly. But the deeper level is understanding. Understanding is not just knowing the regulations in the book, but also the logic of the order, the "why" that sits below the surface. And it is this that is important for trying to use the church order in the life of the church. Very few things happen "by the book," and we cannot force life to fit into the book. The church order serves the church, the church doesn't serve the order. This doesn't mean that we should just permit anything and everything. But the order invites us to be thoughtful in how we operate. Just as important, perhaps even more important, than the answer with which we come up, is how we got there: the leaps and assumptions, the rationales and logic, the theological reflection, and the practical accommodations.

INDEX

Scripture Index

BCO References

Subject and Name Index

ABOUT THE AUTHOR

Matthew J. van Maastricht is the pastor and teacher of the Altamont Reformed Church in Altamont, New York, and a Fellow of the Reformed Church Center and Adjunct Instructor in Reformed Church Studies at New Brunswick Theological Seminary. An internationally known church polity scholar, he is the co-founder of the Society for Protestant Church Polity (https://www.churchpolity.org), and the co-editor of its journal, *Church Polity: International Studies in Protestant Church Polity.* Matthew is currently a PhD candidate in the Faculty of Theology at the Vrije Universiteit Amsterdam.

He has edited two books: *Remembrance, Communion, and Hope: Essays in Honor of Allan J. Janssen*. Historical Series of the Reformed Church in America no. 96 (Grand Rapids, MI: Reformed Church Press, 2019); and *Karl Barth: Theologian in the Tempest of Time* by Karel Blei, and translated by Allan J. Janssen (Eugene, OR: Cascade, 2021) and can be found online at https://churchandorder.org.